201 Woodworking Patterns

*A Bound Set of Useful
and Decorative Woodworking Patterns*

Commit your work to the Lord, then it will succeed.

Proverbs 16:3 The Living Bible

Oh, what a wonderful God we have! How great are his wisdom and knowledge and riches! How impossible it is for us to understand his decisions and his methods! . . . For everything comes from God alone. Everything lives by his power, and everything is for his glory. To him be glory evermore.

Romans 11: 33, 36 The Living Bible

©1990, 1991 Distribution Center
3800 NW 126th Ave.
P.O. Box 8447
Coral Springs, FL 33075

Sixth edition printed January 1992

We have made every effort to ensure the accuracy and completeness of these patterns and drawings. We cannot, however, be responsible for human error, typographical mistakes, or variations in individual work.

ISBN # 0-915099-27-6

Table of Contents

1. Introduction 5

2. Welcomes 9

3. Plaques 19

4. Jewelry 29

5. Clocks 37

6. Modern Art 41

7. Mother Goose & Fairy Tales 43

8. Toys 49

9. Animals 59

10. Christmas 67

11. Holiday, Seasonal & Special Occasions 79

12. Door Harps 93

13. Birdhouses & Yard Birds 97

14. Kitchen Accessories 109

15. Bathroom Accessories..113

16. Projects and Other Useful Accessories......................115

17. Index 159

Introduction

It's happened to you hundreds of times before.

You're in the mall, in a craft store, or at an arts and crafts festival. You see all kinds of wooden household furnishings and decorations that would look great in your house. But, you're just **not** going to spend that much money on something you're **sure** you could make yourself!

You're sure you could make it if you had a pattern, that is.

Problem is, you haven't been able to find any suitable patterns.

Woodworking is one of the fastest-growing and most enjoyable hobbies around in the 1990s.

But woodworkers everywhere have been having real problems finding good patterns. The only patterns that are available on the market today seem to require a college degree in architecture just to understand the instructions. Sound familiar?

Or, if you're lucky enough to find a pattern that isn't written in some complex architect's language, it's usually a pattern that you've already seen or used at least a dozen times. It's been awfully hard to find anything new and creative.

Until now, that is.

We have helped to eliminate this problem. *201 Woodworking Patterns and Designs Encyclopedia* is jam-packed with patterns of all types and for all tastes. Now you **can** make all those things you've seen in the stores!

We have included patterns for the beginner as well as more complex patterns for accomplished woodworkers. And we've given you a wide selection of patterns to choose from.

Some are "golden oldies" — patterns that have been around for some time, but are tried and true winners. Others are fantastic new ideas that you've never seen or even thought of before reading this book!

We believe that, after you thumb through this book, you'll find dozens of projects that you just can't wait to get started on!

But hang on a second!

Before starting your new projects, be sure to read over this next section. We've given you a handful of valuable tips and explanations to make sure your woodworking experience is as exciting and rewarding as you're expecting it to be.

Safety Checklist

Before beginning any project, you always want to make sure you are well protected. Follow all the directions and safety procedures included in the owner's manual that came with your saw.

Always wear safety glasses or goggles to protect your eyes.

If you're wearing a long sleeve shirt, it's a good idea to keep the sleeves rolled up firmly or buttoned around the wrist to keep the material from being pulled into the saw blade.

Make sure you've secured the saw to a workbench or to its own stand so it will not vibrate and fall off while running.

Clear the work area of any extra electrical cords to eliminate the possibility of tripping.

Once you begin working, be sure to feed the wood slowly into the blade with both hands, keeping it pressed firmly against the cutting surface.

Forcing the wood can cause the blade to break or will push the wood off course. Pushing wood into the side of the blade or trying to turn a radius too small for the blade can also break the blade or push it off course.

Tools Required

Choose your tools carefully. The tools that you use will help determine the way your finished project looks. Naturally, high quality tools will perform better and last longer than lower-quality tools.

Of course, the basic tool you'll need is a saw, preferably a power saw.

You have a choice of three types of saws: a scroll saw, a band saw or a jig saw. Each one will work with our patterns. The scroll saw is probably the easiest to work with, but feel free to work with the one that feels the most comfortable to you.

Make sure you keep plenty of extra saw blades on hand. When cutting intricate designs, especially on a scroll saw, the blade could break if too much pressure is applied. So, you'll need a couple of extra blades, just in case.

Also, you need to make sure your saw blades are kept very sharp. Dull blades make for sloppy work and more sanding.

You're also going to need a hammer, tape measure or ruler, sandpaper, sanding block, clamps, drill, drill bits and a good set of screwdrivers. Some of the patterns may suggest using a router. A router is not absolutely necessary, but it would certainly give your projects a nice finishing touch.

Wood

The kind of wood you use for your project will help determine how expensive the project will be. Wood is divided into two basic types: soft and hard.

Soft wood usually comes from the pine family and is less expensive than hard woods. Hard woods include oak, birch and maple.

Wood is also available in different grades, 1, 2 and 3. Grade 1 is the best and the clearest. Classification of wood is determined by its exterior appearance. It is classified as either select or common based.

Select will have little or no defects and will be a little higher priced. Common based is less expensive but may have some defects.

Common based wood is fine to use for your projects as long as the defect is outside of the pattern area. Defects to watch out for are splits, knots or knot holes and warping.

You can buy your wood by the foot. However, most suppliers sell slightly more expensive precut lumber.

The nominal size of lumber is the rough size before it is planed. For example, a 1" x 4" actually measures 3/4" x 3 1/2". The actual size of hard wood, however, is only 1/8" smaller than the nominal dimension, but there is no standard as there is in soft wood. Therefore, a hardwood 1" x 4" measures approximately 7/8" x 3 7/8".

Plywood is good to use for some of the projects. It is better to use larger pieces so no joining is necessary. Plywood is usually sold in 4' x 8' sheets, but it can be bought in smaller sizes. Plywood may also be purchased presanded, so that when you are finishing the piece, only a light sanding will be necessary.

Particle board (a man-made wood) can also be used, but it does not finish well. Consequently, its use should be confined to areas that are not visible.

Luan plywood is inexpensive and finishes well. For most of the patterns that call for 1/4" or thin wood, luan would probably be an acceptable choice. For example: Luan would be a good choice for the Christmas ornaments.

Most of the patterns may be cut from either 1/2" or 3/4" pine with thinner objects being cut from a plywood material and glued on an object to create a 3-D effect. You can choose for yourself what thickness of wood to use.

However, measuring will be very important. If you cut a pattern from 3/4" wood when it calls for 1/2" wood, it will not fit together correctly. Make sure you check your wood sizes and make all necessary adjustments to the pattern before you begin.

Transferring and Enlarging Patterns

There are several different ways to transfer and enlarge patterns. You can experiment with them to see which method you feel most comfortable with.

The first type is the "grid" method. As you will see, some of the patterns in this book are laid out on a grid (like graph paper). The grid is composed of squares, each representing a specified size.

When you get ready to copy the pattern from the book to another sheet of paper, the first thing you need to do is to continue the lines of the grid in the book through the pattern. In other words, extend the lines of the grid through the pattern, so that the pattern has lines drawn through it.

Then get some graph paper or draw another grid on a separate piece of paper. The grid can be as large or as small as you want it to be. If you want the copied pattern to be the same size as the one in the book, make sure the grid squares on your extra piece of paper are the same size as the ones in the book. If you want to make a larger copy of the pattern, make the squares in the grid larger. When you have your grid sized the way you want, simply draw in the same lines that are in the corresponding squares on the pattern in the book.

Another way to enlarge your pattern is through the use of an instrument called a pantograph. A pantograph is an architectural tool — it looks like four long rulers joined together in a zigzag design. This tool can be difficult to work with but is very reliable.

You could also check with your local newspaper office. Newspaper offices usually have enlargement machines, and they may offer pattern enlargement or reduction. The cost will vary depending upon the publisher.

You also may want to consider using photography for pattern enlargement (even though this method could become expensive). You can photograph your pattern using a 35 mm camera with slide film. Then take the developed slide and project the image directly onto a piece of wood or paper and trace it. This method has the advantage of an infinite enlargement range; however, its main drawback is the cost of film and developing.

The last and most popular method of enlargement is photocopying. Many available copiers can reduce or enlarge patterns from 50 –160%. Copy machines can be found just about anywhere — libraries, schools, offices, even the grocery store. Copying is relatively inexpensive, usually just a few cents per page. The most obvious advantage of photocopying is that it may be used for exact pattern transfer as well as for enlargements.

When transferring a pattern to a piece of wood, use tracing paper (available at sewing centers) or carbon paper. Both work the same way. Put the pattern on top of the carbon paper. Then, place the carbon paper on the wood. Trace the pattern, and remove the paper. The image has now been transferred to the wood.

When half patterns are shown in the book (i.e., a heart shape, where each half is exactly the same), fold a piece of paper in half. Draw or trace the half pattern on the paper with the center touching the fold. Cut the pattern on the paper while folded. When opened, the pattern will be perfectly symmetrical.

Cutting the Pattern

You may be thinking that some of the patterns in this book look rather complex. Don't panic! Cutting complex patterns is not as difficult as it appears.

Simply break complicated cuts into simpler curves and lines. Don't be afraid to move your saw to a different position on the wood and approach the line at a different angle.

Look over the piece before beginning each cut. Use a smaller blade to cut curves and corners if there is no way to change the position of your saw and no waste stock to cut into. (Waste stock is simply the extra wood around the pattern.)

If your design calls for sharp corners where two lines intersect, cut the first line and keep going past the corner. Cut a loop around in the waste stock and cut the second line. You can also cut the first line and continue cutting to the edge of

the wood. Take off the waste and turn the piece; then continue cutting from the edge to the second line.

When cutting sharp interior corners, you can cut the first line up to the corner, then back the blade out of the wood and cut the second line.

Another method is to cut the first line up to the corner and back up a few blade widths. Turn into the waste area (leaving the first line) and get in position to cut the second. Cut the second line and take off the waste. Then go back and cut the last part of the second line up to the corner.

When cutting small pieces or very thin veneers, tape your wood to heavy poster board or cardboard (not corrugated cardboard). If the pieces are very thin you can sandwich the wood between two pieces of poster board. This will prevent pieces from breaking or getting lost.

When cutting identical pieces, you could use the pad sawing method. Stack up the wood pieces and tape them together. The stack should not be thicker than the saw cutting capability. Saw the whole stack, then remove the tape. The pieces will be identical.

Gluing

For pieces that will be kept indoors, use a white polyvinyl glue or a yellow aliphatic resin. Elmer's wood glue is an excellent choice for indoor use. Outdoor projects require a waterproof glue such as resorcinol or epoxy.

Before you begin gluing, make sure the surfaces to be glued are smooth, dry and free from oil or grease. Clean surfaces take glue much easier than dirty ones.

Apply the glue, then clamp the wood together tightly. Allow plenty of time for the glue to set and dry completely. Manufacturers usually specify drying times on the glue container.

If you're going to stain your finished project, make sure no glue comes out of the seams. Excess dried glue on the wood surface will prevent proper color absorption into the wood.

Finishing

After you've completely finished cutting out your project, the project is ready to be "finished".

First, sand the piece with a rough grade of sandpaper (100-200 grit). Then sand again with finer paper or emery cloth (up to 500 grit) until the piece is smooth. Steel wool (0000 or 4-0) is best for the final sanding and for smoothing bubbles between coats of finish or polyurethane.

There are several different ways to finish the piece. It can be painted, stained, stenciled or finished with tung oil.

If you've decided to paint your project, make sure you use top quality paint brushes made of camel hair or other natural fibers. Applicators on wooden handles are better because they don't leave brush marks. You also may use a power sprayer to get a clean finished surface. And it's always a good idea to keep several lint-free rags handy for clean up as well as for applying stains and sealers.

Acrylic paints are easy to use and easy to clean up. Rinsing with plain water and soap will clean brushes thoroughly. You may decide to buy and use a brush cleaner that contains a conditioner which will help keep your brushes more supple and make them last longer. After acrylic paints have dried on the wood surface, they make a permanent waterproof surface.

If you're feeling a little unsure about your ability to paint your projects, don't worry. You're not alone! We've found that many people who feel very comfortable with a saw in their hands suddenly feel very awkward when they pick up a paint brush. For this very reason, there are many publications in craft, hobby or discount stores on painting.

The most popular type of painting for wooden pieces is tole painting. This is an easy method of applying paint in layers with common designs and shading techniques. Tole painting is probably simpler for a beginner than any other type of painting, and, with practice, patience and the proper instructions, anyone can master this technique. You'll find that a large variety of tole painting books are available in craft and hobby shops everywhere. In fact, many of the patterns included in this book already have designs suitable for tole painting.

You may decide that your project would look best with a stenciled design instead of tole-painted designs. Stenciling is the art of dabbing paint, ink or dye through openings in a piece of plastic or cardboard, leaving an impression behind.

Stenciling has become very popular these days, and if it's done properly, it can make a beautiful piece. You can buy all kinds of stencil patterns in craft shops — from flowers and leaves to barnyard animals to hearts and angels.

Once you've decided on your stencil pattern, tape the pattern down to the wood surface. (You may want to practice stenciling on paper before you attempt painting on the wooden piece, just to make sure it's going to turn out the way you're hoping it will.)

The "dry brush" method of stenciling works best. Too much paint on your brush will run or drip. You can use brushes, sponges or spray paint to stencil.

A new product on the market is a stick paint. Stick paints look very much like large crayons, and you "color" with them the same way you color with crayons. The stick application is very easy, and it involves less mess than other methods. Another advantage of using stick paints is that they don't run like paint does when you use the brush application. For this reason, it is widely becoming the favorite of many first-time stencilers.

Staining is another popular finish for wooden pieces. You can get many different shades and colors of stain in craft shops and hardware stores. Just make sure you test your stain on a piece of scrap wood to check the color before putting it on the wooden piece.

Stain is very easy to apply. You can apply it with a brush, or you can wipe it on with a lint-free soft cloth. Wipe the stain on with the grain of the wood, then against the grain. Wipe off the excess with the grain.

After staining, rub the piece with 0000 grit sand paper. Brush on a coat of polyurethane over the dried stain, brushing along with the grain, forcing out the bubbles. After it has dried thoroughly, follow with a steel-wool rub to eliminate any bubbles that may have formed.

For best results, use a tacky cloth (found at paint stores and in the hardware section of most discount stores) to remove dust after each sanding. Polyurethane forms a hard, bright, waterproof finish. It comes in a high gloss or satin finish. Make sure you are in a well-ventilated, dust-free environment when applying polyurethane.

Tung oil is also a great finish. Tung oil is a thick, heavy liquid applied directly to the wood by hand or with a lint-free cloth. Several coats form a water- and stain-resistant finish. A coat of polyurethane over the dried tung oil will protect the surface even more.

Miscellaneous Needs

Before you begin, you'll find that you're going to need a few more items to help you get started on your new projects. Make sure you always check your pattern before you begin so that you will not have to stop and make an inconvenient trip to the store for that one item that you forgot.

Here's a list of some additional items we recommend for the patterns in this book:

Plenty of sharpened #2 pencils
Twine or ribbon for certain patterns
Dowel rods of various sizes
An assortment of nails, especially small finishing nails
Wood putty to cover up nail holes for finishing
Hinges and fasteners as indicated by patterns
Cup hooks, L-hooks and coat hangers — available at hardware stores
Shaker pegs

Use your creativity and imagination! Most of the patterns include specific instructions for a certain design, but you can easily change the patterns. If a pattern in the book sparks your imagination for a slightly different design or finish, then go for it! Don't hesitate to branch out and try your own ideas. These patterns can be mixed and matched, changed and rearranged to provide you with a limitless supply of ideas and hours of fun and enjoyment.

Welcomes

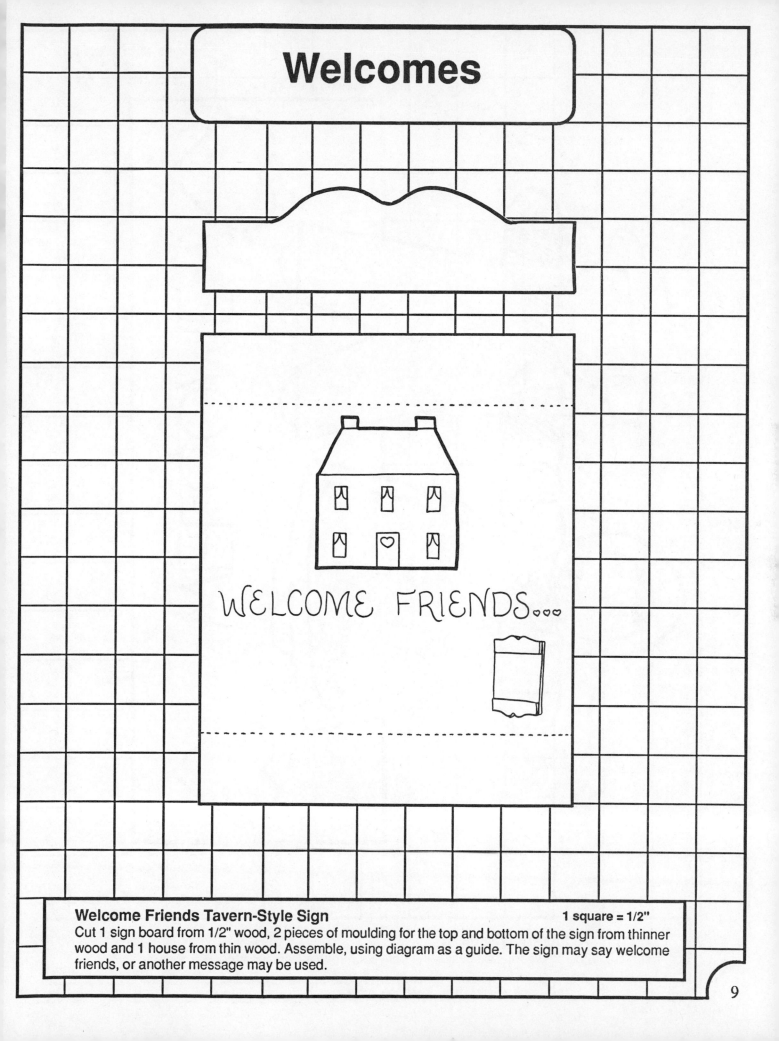

Welcome Friends Tavern-Style Sign   **1 square = 1/2"**

Cut 1 sign board from 1/2" wood, 2 pieces of moulding for the top and bottom of the sign from thinner wood and 1 house from thin wood. Assemble, using diagram as a guide. The sign may say welcome friends, or another message may be used.

An Amish Country Welcome
Cut out from 1/2" wood. Use beside the front door or anywhere for a friendly, country look.

1 square = 3/4"

11

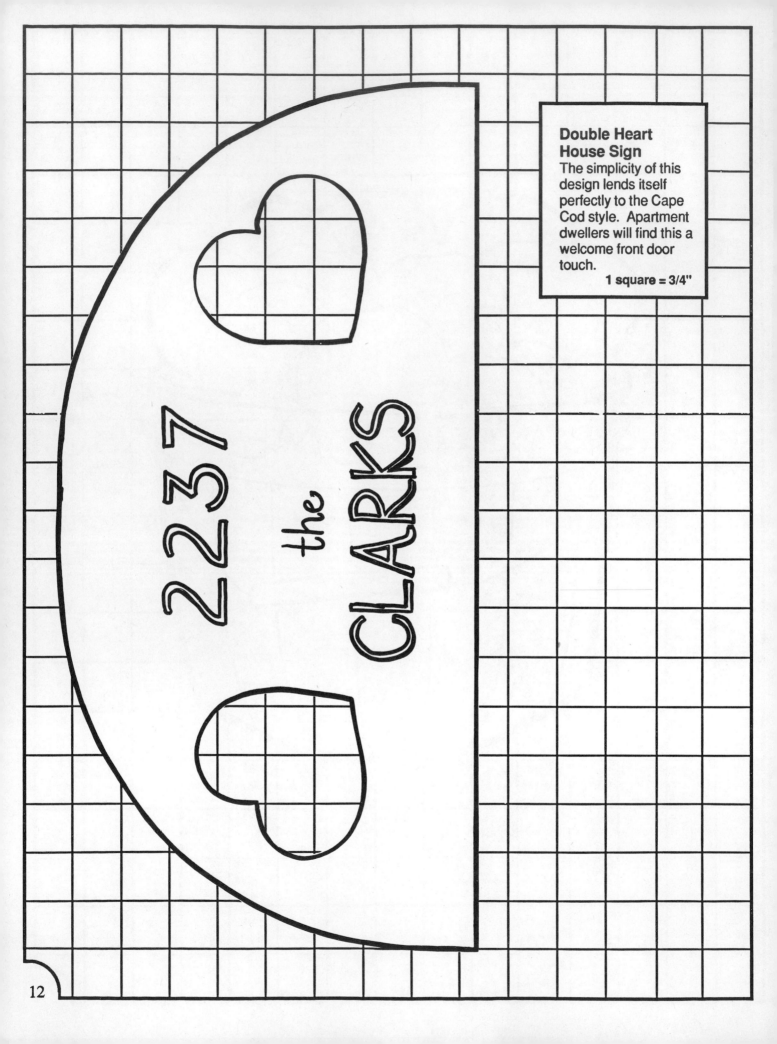

Double Heart House Sign
The simplicity of this design lends itself perfectly to the Cape Cod style. Apartment dwellers will find this a welcome front door touch.

1 square = 3/4"

2237

the
CLARKS

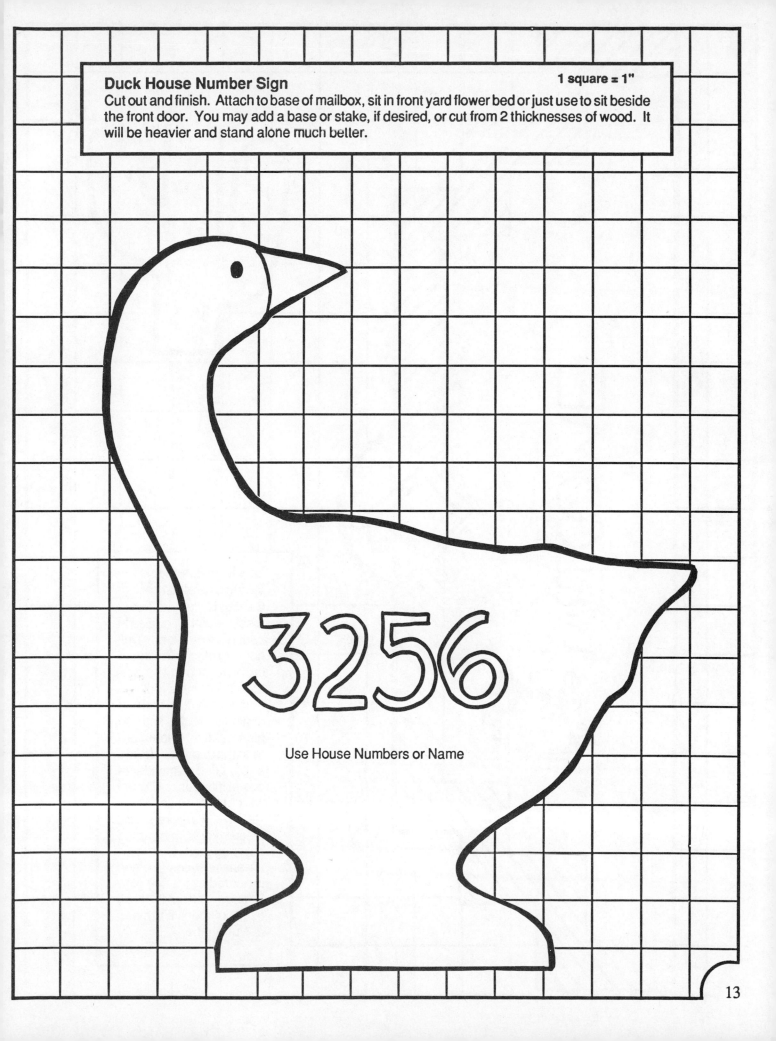

Duck House Number Sign

Cut out and finish. Attach to base of mailbox, sit in front yard flower bed or just use to sit beside the front door. You may add a base or stake, if desired, or cut from 2 thicknesses of wood. It will be heavier and stand alone much better.

1 square = 1"

3256

Use House Numbers or Name

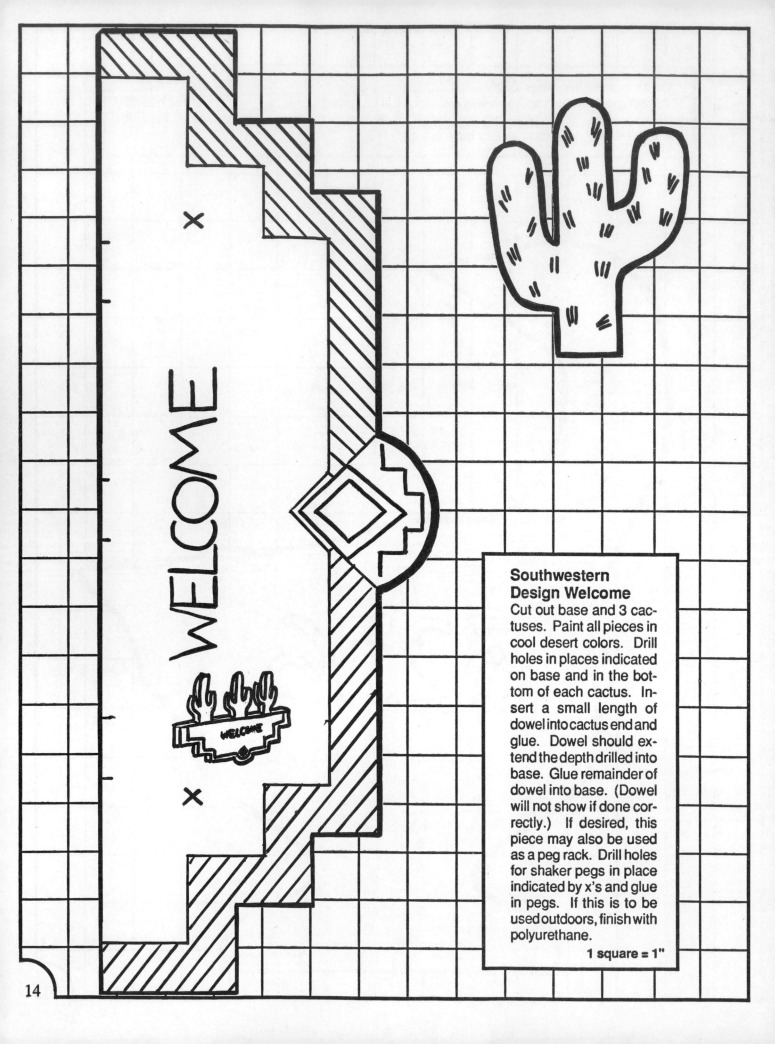

WELCOME

Southwestern Design Welcome

Cut out base and 3 cactuses. Paint all pieces in cool desert colors. Drill holes in places indicated on base and in the bottom of each cactus. Insert a small length of dowel into cactus end and glue. Dowel should extend the depth drilled into base. Glue remainder of dowel into base. (Dowel will not show if done correctly.) If desired, this piece may also be used as a peg rack. Drill holes for shaker pegs in place indicated by x's and glue in pegs. If this is to be used outdoors, finish with polyurethane.

1 square = 1"

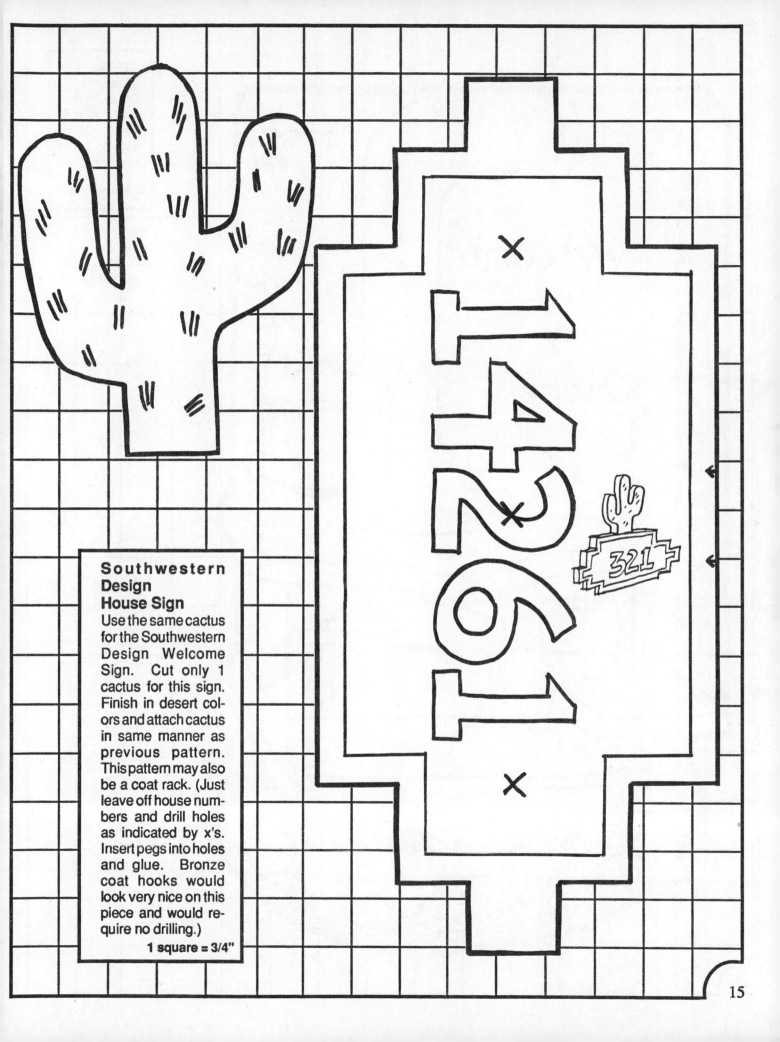

Southwestern Design House Sign

Use the same cactus for the Southwestern Design Welcome Sign. Cut only 1 cactus for this sign. Finish in desert colors and attach cactus in same manner as previous pattern. This pattern may also be a coat rack. (Just leave off house numbers and drill holes as indicated by x's. Insert pegs into holes and glue. Bronze coat hooks would look very nice on this piece and would require no drilling.)

1 square = 3/4"

Welcome
to
my
Kitchen

Cozy Kitchen Welcome
Cut out from 1/2" wood. Finish using acrylic paint and hang.

1 square = 3/4"

WELCOME

to my KITCHEN

Kitchen Canning Welcome
Cut out from 1/2" wood. Finish with acrylic paints and hang in kitchen.

Actual Size

Front Door House Number Sign

Cut out from 1/2" or 3/4" wood. Cut out or paint on heart. It might be easier to paint the ivy design first and paint the numbers over the ivy. Either stain background or paint white or a light color.

Actual Size

18

Plaques

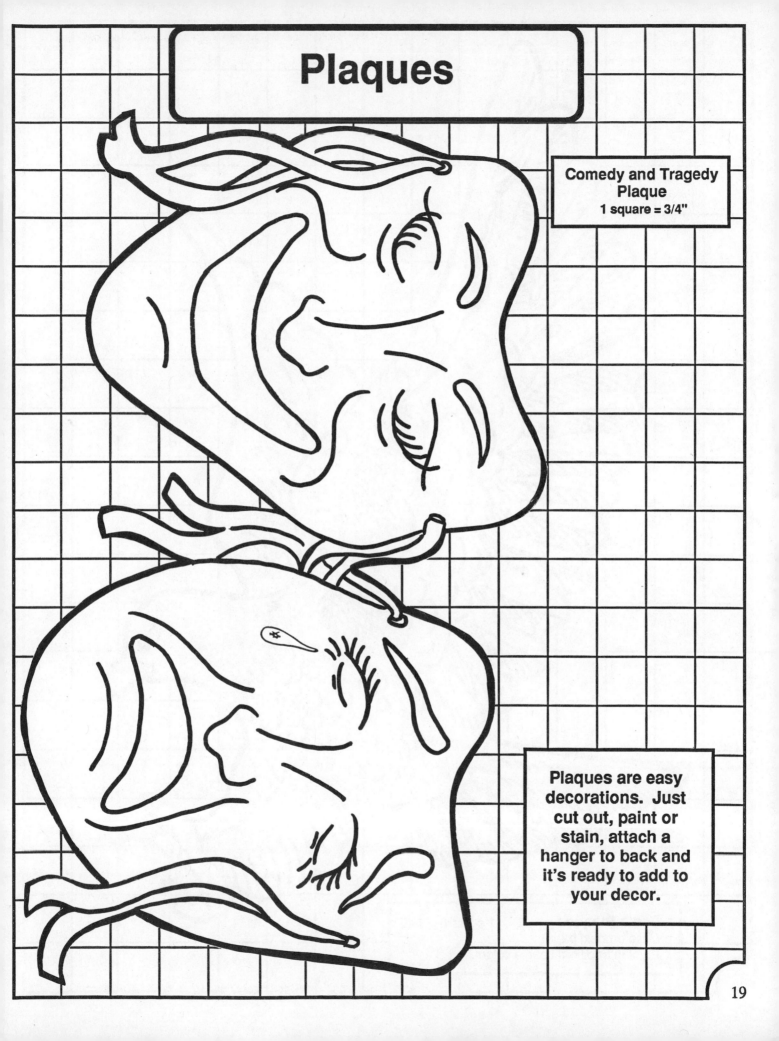

Comedy and Tragedy Plaque
1 square = 3/4"

Plaques are easy decorations. Just cut out, paint or stain, attach a hanger to back and it's ready to add to your decor.

19

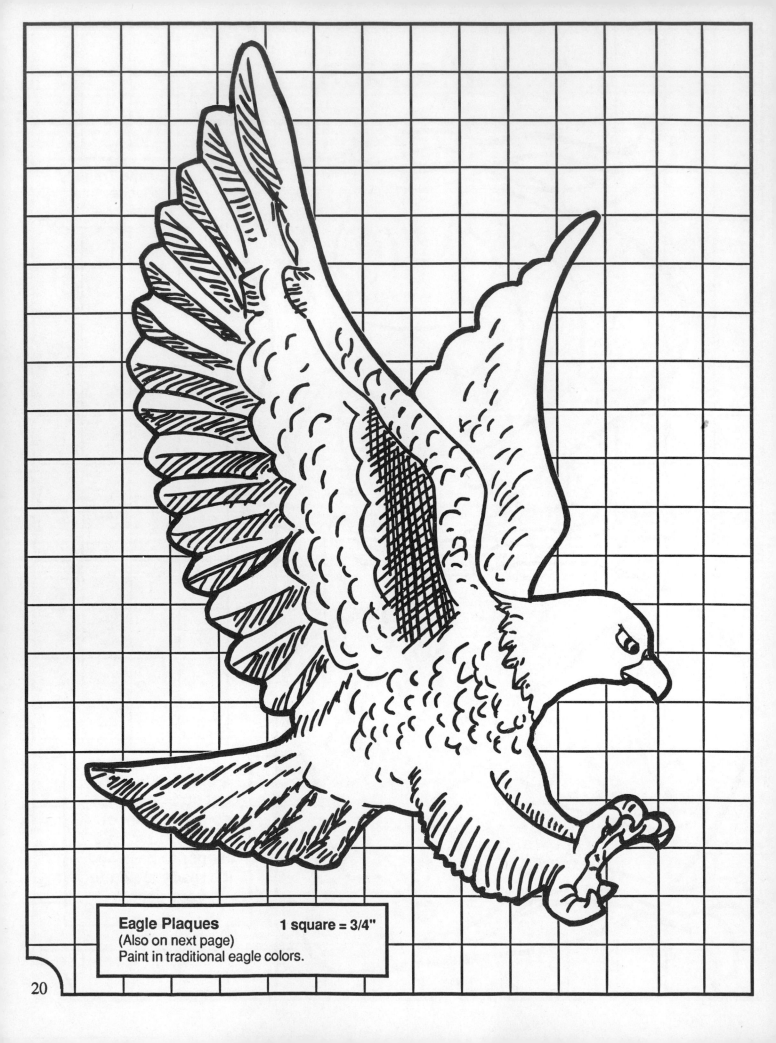

Eagle Plaques   1 square = 3/4"
(Also on next page)
Paint in traditional eagle colors.

20

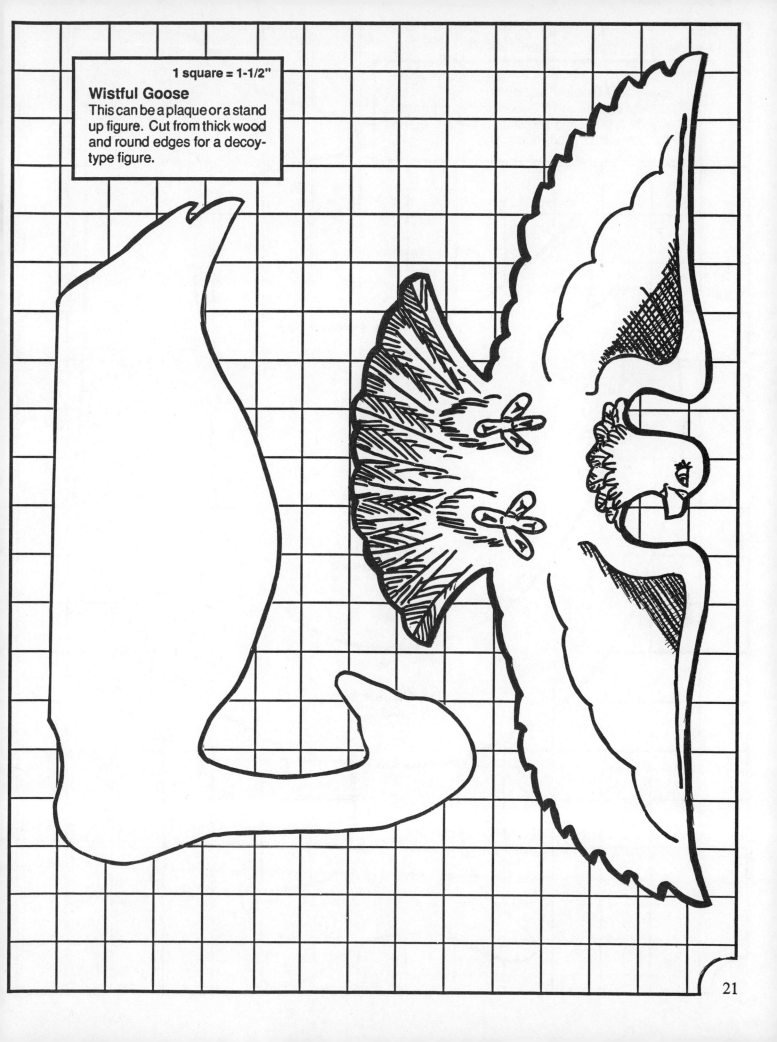

1 square = 1-1/2"

Wistful Goose
This can be a plaque or a stand up figure. Cut from thick wood and round edges for a decoy-type figure.

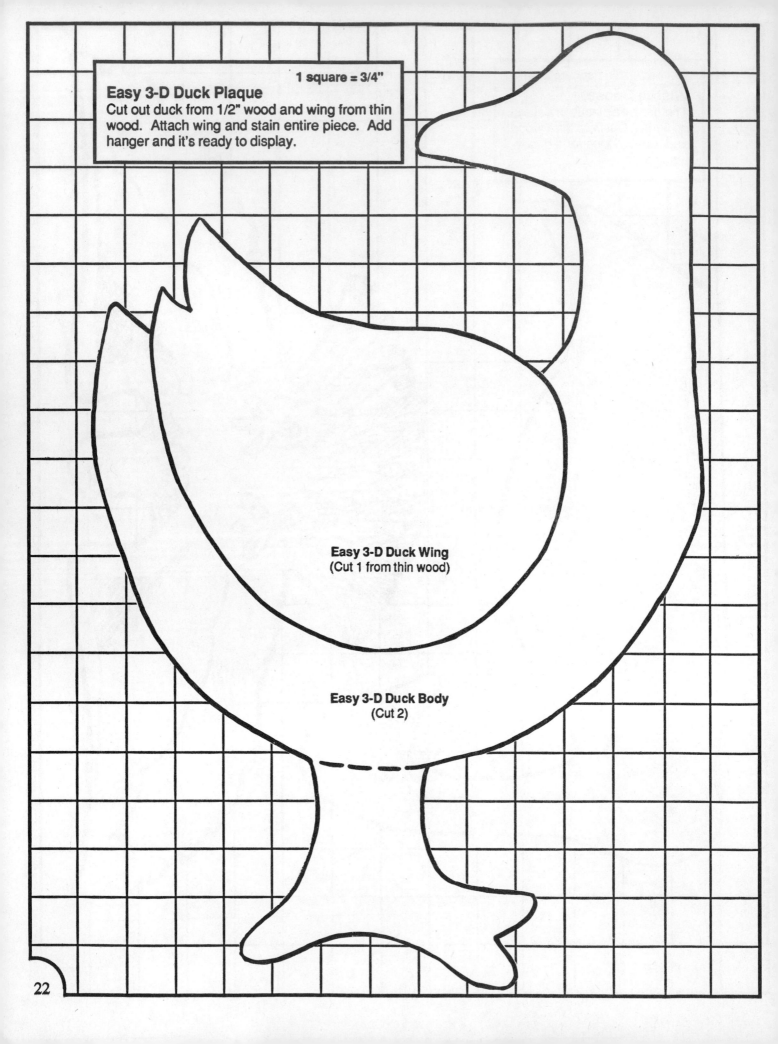

1 square = 3/4"

Easy 3-D Duck Plaque
Cut out duck from 1/2" wood and wing from thin wood. Attach wing and stain entire piece. Add hanger and it's ready to display.

Easy 3-D Duck Wing
(Cut 1 from thin wood)

Easy 3-D Duck Body
(Cut 2)

22

Mexican Pitcher Wall Plaque
1 square = 3/4"

23

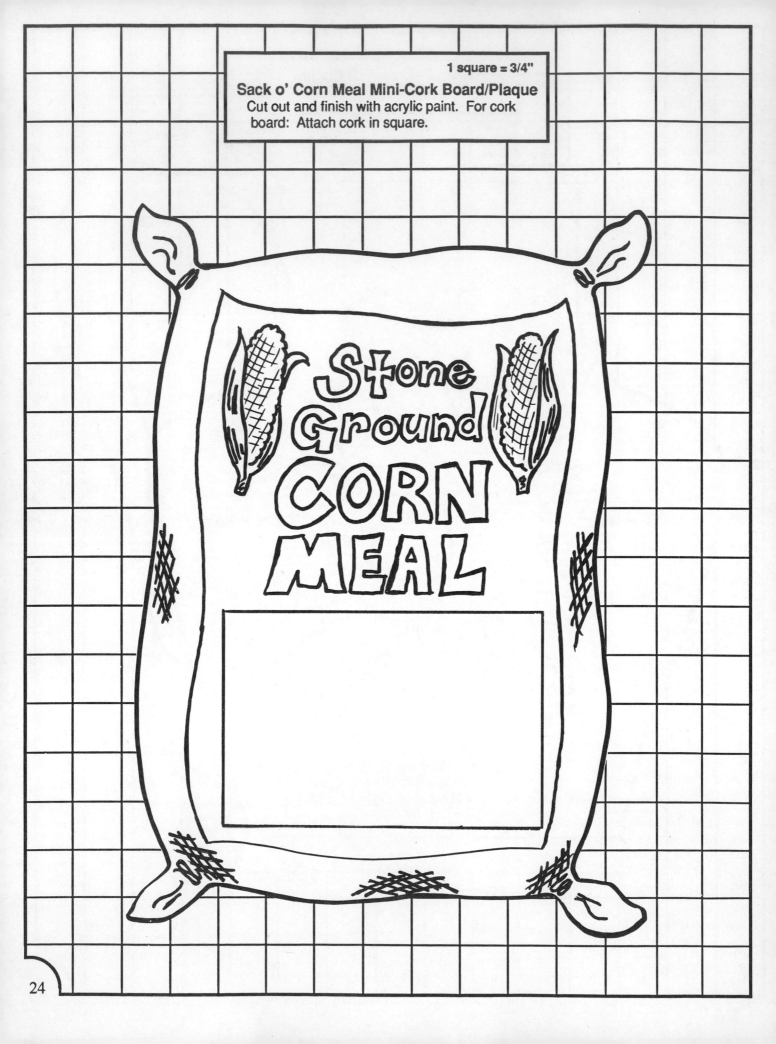

1 square = 3/4"

Sack o' Corn Meal Mini-Cork Board/Plaque
Cut out and finish with acrylic paint. For cork board: Attach cork in square.

Stone Ground CORN MEAL

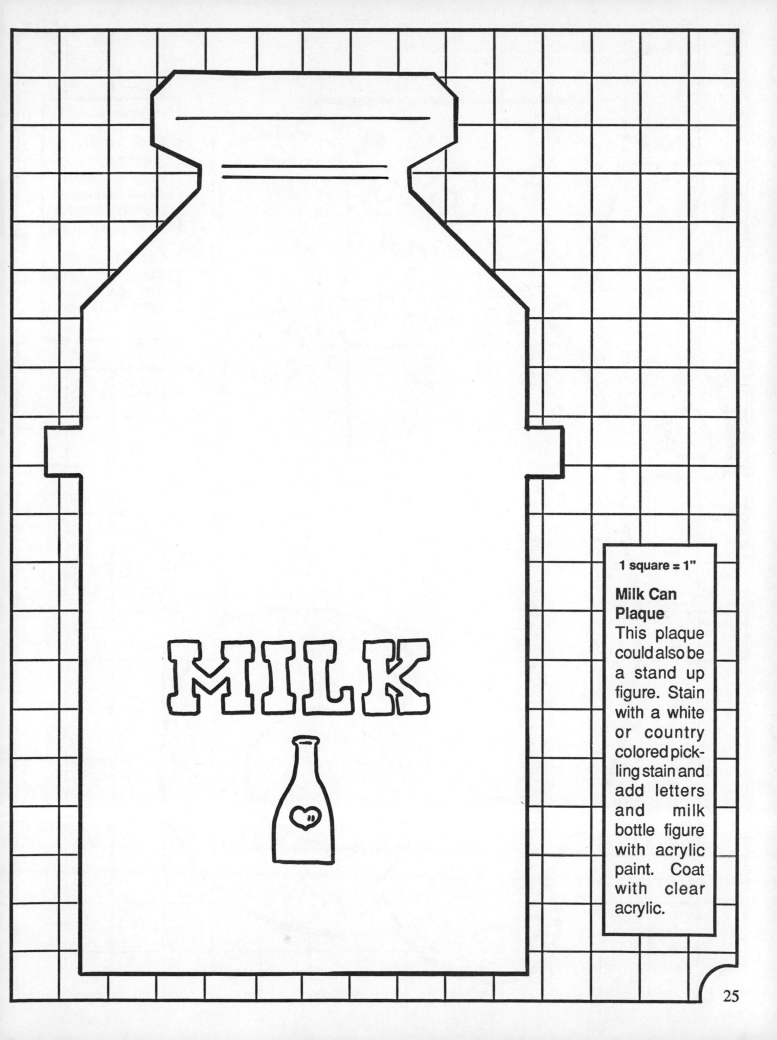

MILK

1 square = 1"

Milk Can Plaque
This plaque could also be a stand up figure. Stain with a white or country colored pickling stain and add letters and milk bottle figure with acrylic paint. Coat with clear acrylic.

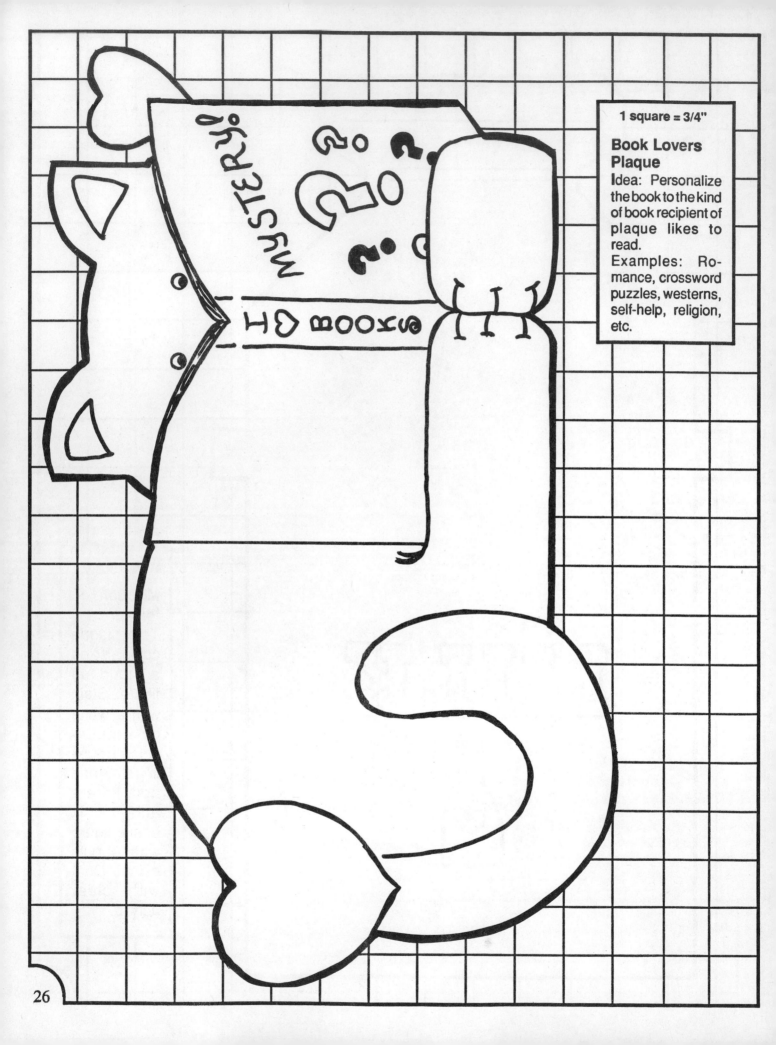

MYSTERY!

? ? ?
? ? ?

I ♥ BOOKS

1 square = 3/4"

Book Lovers Plaque
Idea: Personalize the book to the kind of book recipient of plaque likes to read.
Examples: Romance, crossword puzzles, westerns, self-help, religion, etc.

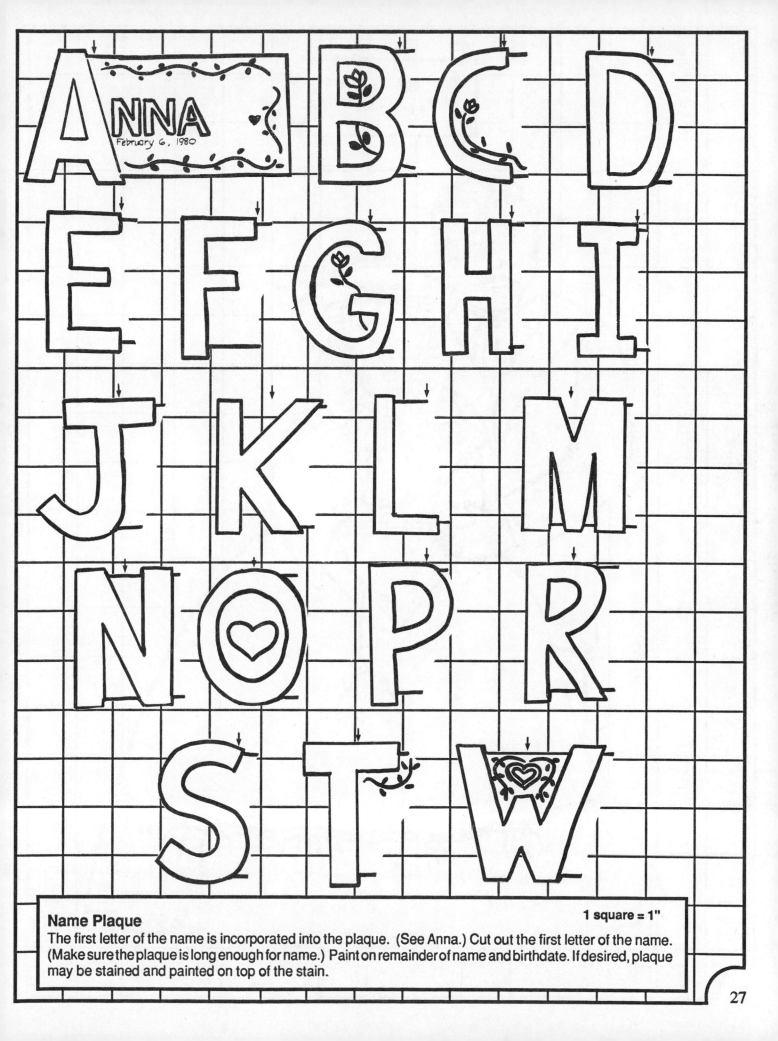

Name Plaque

The first letter of the name is incorporated into the plaque. (See Anna.) Cut out the first letter of the name. (Make sure the plaque is long enough for name.) Paint on remainder of name and birthdate. If desired, plaque may be stained and painted on top of the stain.

1 square = 1"

Victorian Lady & Gent
1 square = 3/4"

28

Jewelry

Necklace

Cut each piece. Make sure that wood is thick enough to drill through. (1/2" wood is the desirable width, but thinner wood could be used if drilling is possible.) Drill through each piece where indicated by ribbon. Paint and string all pieces on ribbon, alternating with beads where indicated. Beads should be tied in place with knots so they will not move. Ribbon is normally used, but rawhide may be used in this design.

Belt Buckle

Cut out and finish. Use as buckle for belt or use western style handkerchief for belt.

Earrings

(Cut 2 from thin wood)
Flip Pattern to cut left earring.
Cut small angular shapes by pattern (as shown) or use jewels in the same shapes. Finish and glue shapes or jewels to front. Glue earring backs on. Glue close to top so that earrings will hang correctly.

Barrette Cover

Cut out of thin wood, finish and glue cover to barrette.

Classy Southwestern Contemporary Jewelry Ensemble

Cut out each piece and finish before assembly. Barrettes, pin backs, earring backs, beads, jewels and ribbon may be purchased at craft and hobby stores or in the craft section of your local discount stores. This type of jewelry is very popular and will last indefinitely. Paint in browns, mauves and blacks or in cool desert colors.

Fashion Pin

(Cut 1 base and 1 triangle from thin wood) Cut one pin base and one triangle. Drill small hole for ribbon (or rawhide) and beads. Paint as indicated. Attach beads last. Glue to pin.

Skater Pin

Make arms and legs out of heavy fashion wire and attach beads at ends. Drill small holes for legs and arms. Insert wire and fasten with hot glue. Attach pin to back with hot glue.

Scarf Slide

Cut out large and small triangle. Drill small hole for ribbon or rawhide and beads.

Tee-Pull

Cut out and finish. Drill three small holes for ribbons or rawhide and beads. Pull corner of Tee Shirt through and tie a knot in shirt to hold in place.

Mad Dog Tee-Pull

Cut out and finish. Pull Tee Shirt through hole and knot.

30

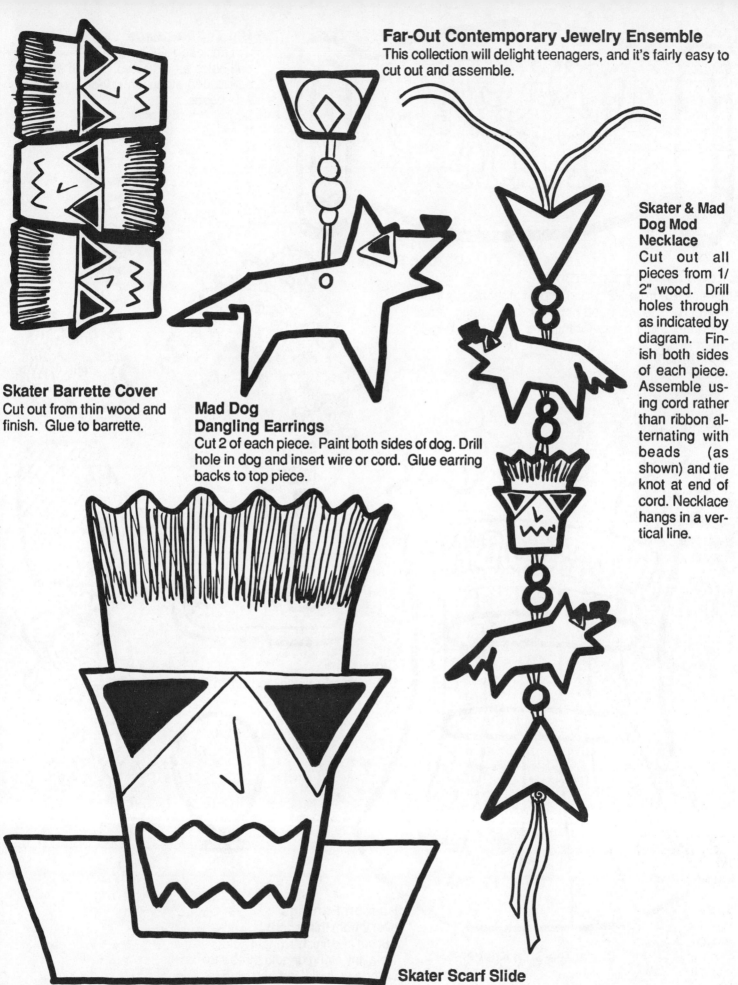

Far-Out Contemporary Jewelry Ensemble
This collection will delight teenagers, and it's fairly easy to cut out and assemble.

Skater & Mad Dog Mod Necklace
Cut out all pieces from 1/2" wood. Drill holes through as indicated by diagram. Finish both sides of each piece. Assemble using cord rather than ribbon alternating with beads (as shown) and tie knot at end of cord. Necklace hangs in a vertical line.

Skater Barrette Cover
Cut out from thin wood and finish. Glue to barrette.

Mad Dog Dangling Earrings
Cut 2 of each piece. Paint both sides of dog. Drill hole in dog and insert wire or cord. Glue earring backs to top piece.

Skater Scarf Slide

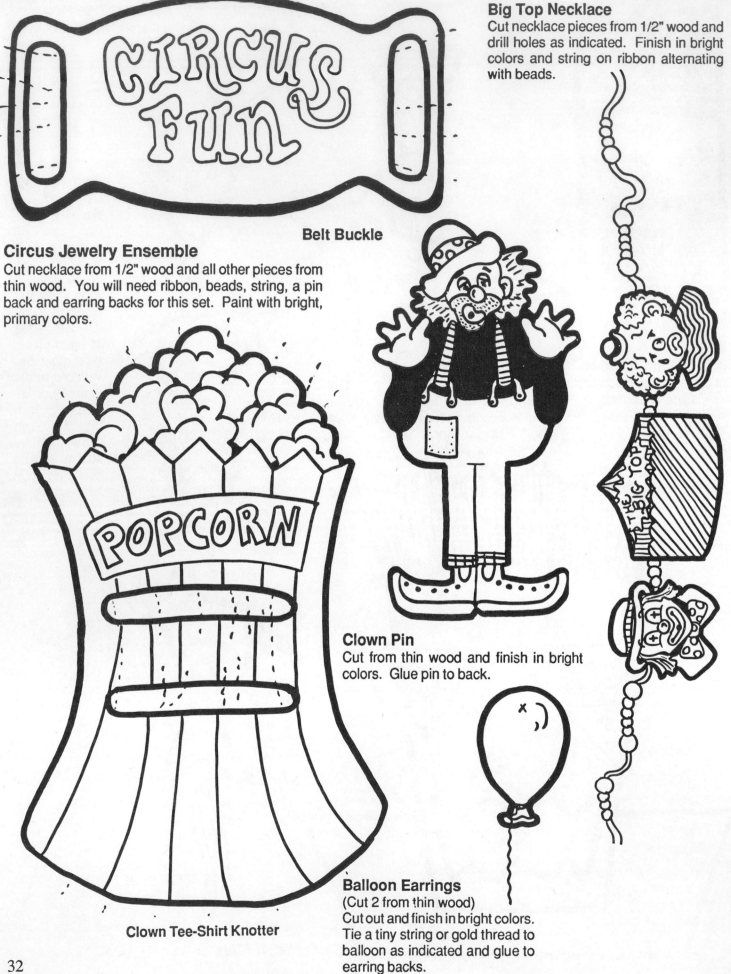

CIRCUS FUN

Big Top Necklace
Cut necklace pieces from 1/2" wood and drill holes as indicated. Finish in bright colors and string on ribbon alternating with beads.

Belt Buckle

Circus Jewelry Ensemble
Cut necklace from 1/2" wood and all other pieces from thin wood. You will need ribbon, beads, string, a pin back and earring backs for this set. Paint with bright, primary colors.

POPCORN

Clown Pin
Cut from thin wood and finish in bright colors. Glue pin to back.

Clown Tee-Shirt Knotter

Balloon Earrings
(Cut 2 from thin wood)
Cut out and finish in bright colors. Tie a tiny string or gold thread to balloon as indicated and glue to earring backs.

Noah's Ark Jewelry Ensemble

Cut necklace pieces out of 1/2" wood and all other pieces from thin wood. This set calls for ribbon, earring backs and a pin back.

Circular Rainbow Tee-Shirt Knotter

Cut from thin wood and finish in rainbow colors. Pull Tee-shirt through hole and tie a knot in end.

Noah and Friends Fashion Folk Pin

Cut from thin wood and finish using natural colors. Glue pin to back.

Noah's Cow Earrings

(Cut two)
Finish and glue to earring backs.

Good News Dove Scarf Slide

Reversible: Ascending or Descending. Cut from thin wood and finish as shown.

Noah's Ark Necklace

Cut each piece from 1/2" wood and drill holes as indicated. Finish as shown using natural colors. Assemble using ribbon and alternating each piece with beads in primary rainbow colors.

33

Rudolph Jewelry Ensemble

This cute jewelry set will delight everyone at Christmas. In addition to red or green ribbon, earring backs and beads you will need two small red pom-poms and small jingle bells.

Rudolph Fashion Necklace

Cut 1 Rudolph and 2 Christmas balls from 1/2" wood. Drill holes as indicated for ribbon. Finish and attach red pom-pom to nose and jingle bells on balls with hot glue. To assemble, string on ribbon alternately with beads. Rudolph should be brown with golden or light brown antlers and light brown inside ears. Bow tie should be red with green Christmas trees with brown trunks. Use black for eyes and detailing.

Rudolph Fashion Pin

Cut out and finish using same colors as necklace. Glue bell on back where indicated by x. Glue small red pom-pom for nose. Glue pin to back.

Rudolph's Bow Tie Single Hole Tee-Pull

Cut 1 from thin wood.

Rudolph's Bow Tie Earrings

Cut 2 from thin wood and finish. Glue to earring backs.

Christmas Ball Belt Buckle

Cut out and finish. Glue small jingle bells on x's or drill small holes and attach bells with wire.

Wise Men Jewelry Ensemble
For this set you will need ribbon, earring backs, and a pin back. Wise men should be cut from 1/2" wood. All others from thin wood. Paint in jewel tones.

Wise Men Necklace
Cut out each piece from 1/2" wood and drill hole in top 1/3 of each piece to prevent from flipping. Finish as indicated in jewel tones. Assemble on burgundy, deep rose or emerald ribbon, alternating with matching beads.

Manger Fashion Pin
Cut out manger and star separately. Finish and hang star with gold thread. Attach pin to back at the top of piece.

Myrrh Decanter Earrings
Cut out from thin wood and finish in jewel tones. Glue to earring backs.

Wise Man Tee Pull
Cut out from thin wood and finish in jewel tones.

Frankincense Scarf Slide
Cut out from thin wood and finish in jewel tones.

Bear Necklace

Cut out 3 bears from 1/2" wood. Drill hole in top 1/3 of each piece. Finish and string, alternating with beads.

Scottie and Bows Necklace

Cut 1 scottie and 2 bows for each necklace from 1/2" wood. Drill holes for ribbon and finish both sides. Scottie should be black with name in red letters. Bows should be red with black detailing. Use red ribbon to string. Tie knots between each piece to keep in place. For matching earrings: Cut 2 bows from thin wood and finish one side. Glue to earring backs.

Bunny and Carrot Earrings

Cut out 1 bunny and 2 carrots from 1/2" wood. Drill holes in top 1/3 of each piece. Finish both sides. (Bunny should be white and carrots orange with green tops. Detailing should be done with black or dark brown.) String on peach or white ribbon.

Fruit Necklace

Cut out each piece and finish both sides. Drill holes in top 1/3 of each piece and string on brightly colored ribbon.

Clocks

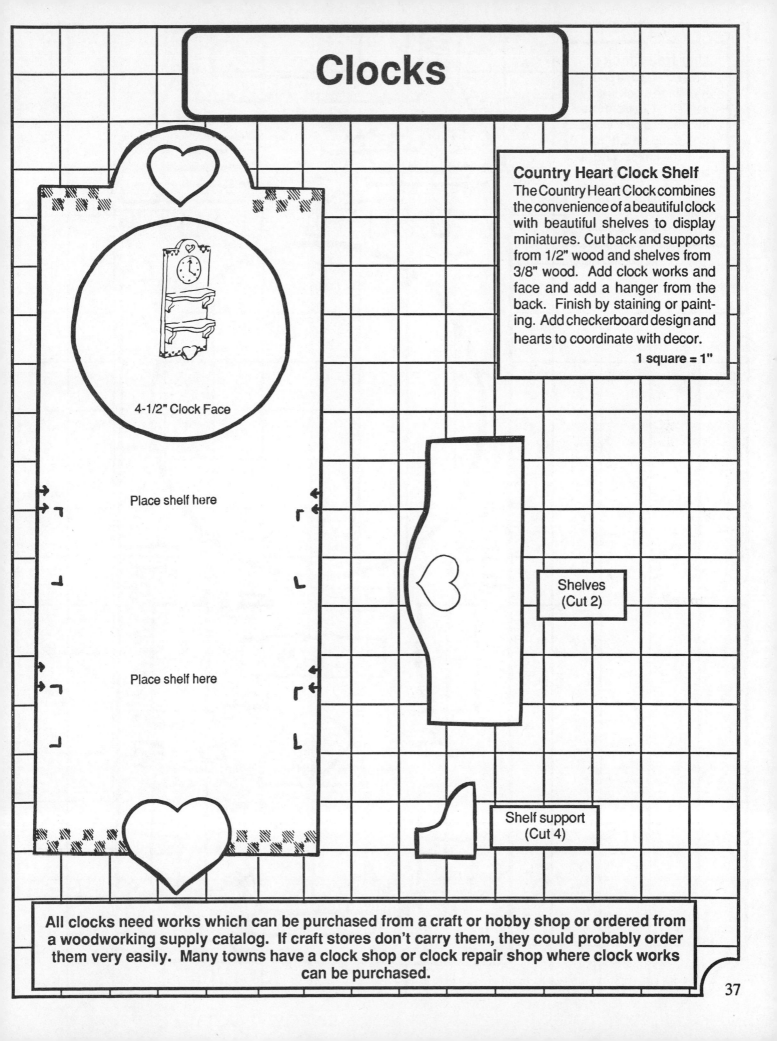

Country Heart Clock Shelf
The Country Heart Clock combines the convenience of a beautiful clock with beautiful shelves to display miniatures. Cut back and supports from 1/2" wood and shelves from 3/8" wood. Add clock works and face and add a hanger from the back. Finish by staining or painting. Add checkerboard design and hearts to coordinate with decor.

1 square = 1"

4-1/2" Clock Face

Place shelf here

Place shelf here

Shelves
(Cut 2)

Shelf support
(Cut 4)

All clocks need works which can be purchased from a craft or hobby shop or ordered from a woodworking supply catalog. If craft stores don't carry them, they could probably order them very easily. Many towns have a clock shop or clock repair shop where clock works can be purchased.

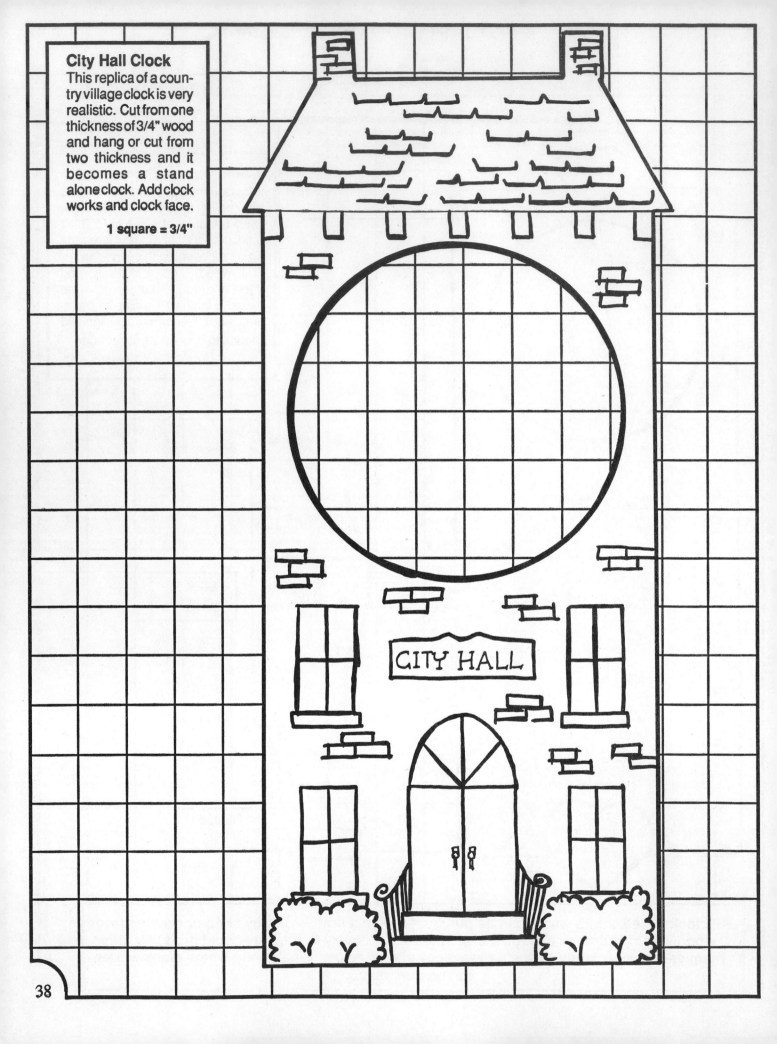

City Hall Clock
This replica of a country village clock is very realistic. Cut from one thickness of 3/4" wood and hang or cut from two thickness and it becomes a stand alone clock. Add clock works and clock face.

1 square = 3/4"

CITY HALL

Welcome Heart Clock
This clock, hanging in a foyer or entranceway makes a pleasant, convenient greeting for guests. Cut from 3/4" wood. Add clock works. Paint on face or put on bought face. Add hanger and it's ready to display.

1 square = 3/4"

39

Ask any kid what time it is and he'll tell you that it's always time for cookies. This cookie jar clock will be very popular with kid's of all ages. Cut from 3/4" wood, add clock works and hang in the kitchen.

TIME FOR

4-1/2" Clock Face

COOKIES

Modern Art

Attached leg

X
Bolt "Attached leg" here

Moveable Ultraman Modern Sculpture   **1 square = 1"**

All pieces are shown assembled. The bold lines are the cutting lines. To cut out trace individual pieces on wood and cut out (there are 10 pieces to this pattern including the stand). The torso is one piece and the right leg is one piece. Attach all pieces together with dowel or brads. The arms, head and one leg should be "moveable". Attach right leg to base as indicated.

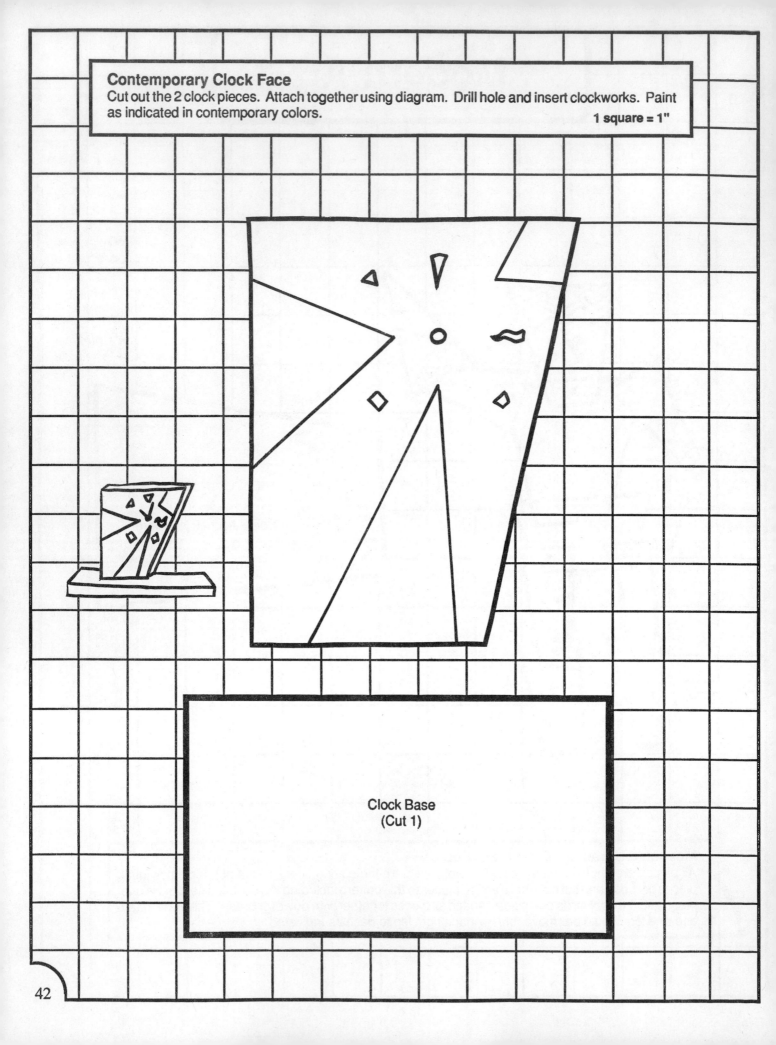

Contemporary Clock Face
Cut out the 2 clock pieces. Attach together using diagram. Drill hole and insert clockworks. Paint as indicated in contemporary colors.

1 square = 1"

Clock Base
(Cut 1)

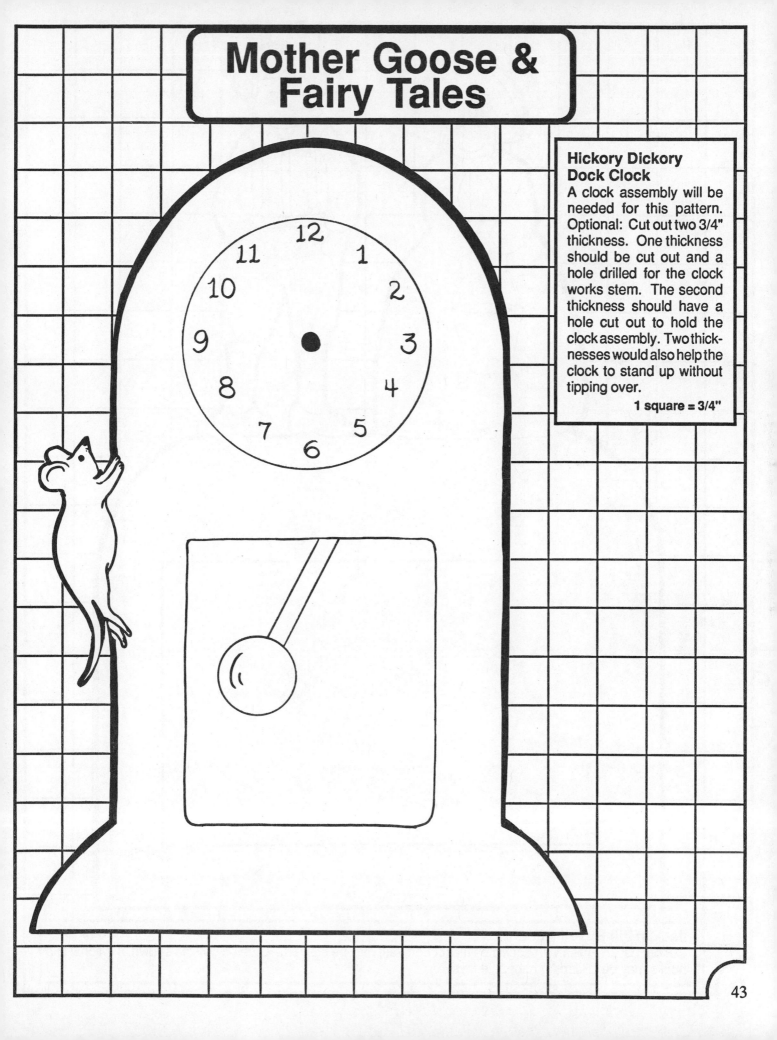

Mother Goose & Fairy Tales

Hickory Dickory Dock Clock

A clock assembly will be needed for this pattern. Optional: Cut out two 3/4" thickness. One thickness should be cut out and a hole drilled for the clock works stem. The second thickness should have a hole cut out to hold the clock assembly. Two thicknesses would also help the clock to stand up without tipping over.

1 square = 3/4"

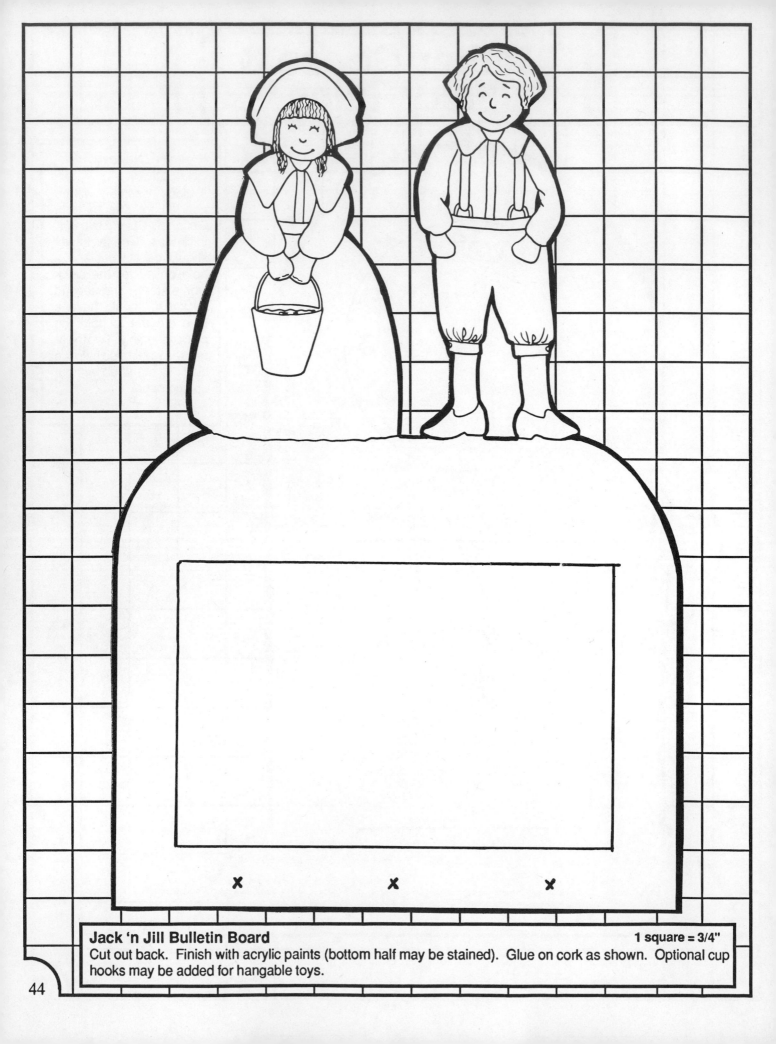

Jack 'n Jill Bulletin Board
Cut out back. Finish with acrylic paints (bottom half may be stained). Glue on cork as shown. Optional cup hooks may be added for hangable toys.

1 square = 3/4"

44

**Rub-A-Dub-Dub Bathroom
Multi-Purpose Peg**
Place a peg as indicated by an X.
Use for hanging robe, towel,
jewelry, shower cap, etc.

45

Shelf Support
(Cut three)

Little Bo Peep Wall Shelf
Cut out one shelf back, one shelf and three shelf supports. Assemble shelf and finish with acrylic paints.

1 square = 1"

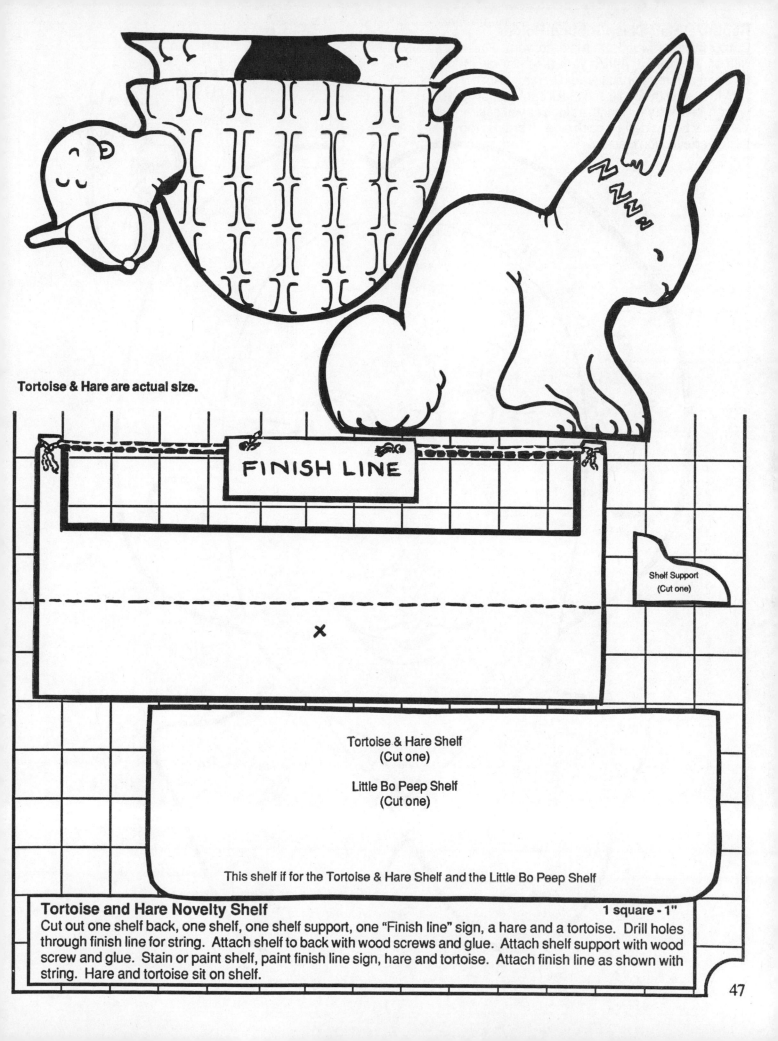

Tortoise & Hare are actual size.

FINISH LINE

Shelf Support
(Cut one)

×

Tortoise & Hare Shelf
(Cut one)

Little Bo Peep Shelf
(Cut one)

This shelf if for the Tortoise & Hare Shelf and the Little Bo Peep Shelf

Tortoise and Hare Novelty Shelf

1 square - 1"

Cut out one shelf back, one shelf, one shelf support, one "Finish line" sign, a hare and a tortoise. Drill holes through finish line for string. Attach shelf to back with wood screws and glue. Attach shelf support with wood screw and glue. Stain or paint shelf, paint finish line sign, hare and tortoise. Attach finish line as shown with string. Hare and tortoise sit on shelf.

47

Rapunzel Hair Clasp/Ribbon Holder

Cut out from 3/4" wood. Drill holes for yarn. Finish with acrylic paints. Attach yarn (see diagrams). String yarn through back (see diagram). Anchor yarn in back with hot glue so that it can't be pulled apart. Make the yarn length as long as you desire. Yarn may be braided on each side. If braid is too thick, barrette won't fasten.

48

Toys

Farmer

Farm Goose

Sitting Dog

Farmer's Wife

Farm Boy

Farm Girl

Grandma

Grandpa

Bale of Hay

Barn Owl

Farm Mule

Farm Pig

Attach wire

Farm Bucket

Farm Play Set With Barn (Barn Holder/Carrier on pages 51 & 52)
Cut out all farm pieces from 3/4" wood. Paint all farm pieces on front and back. It is very hard to carry the design over the cut out edge. It would be a good idea to paint around the edge with black or beige or a neutral color. This farm set will give young children many hours of creative enjoyment. Make sure not to give the smallest pieces to children under three (especially the farm hen which could be swallowed by very young children.)

49

Farm Cat

Farm Duck

Rabbit

Farm Turkey

Lazy Farm Dog

Lazy Farm Pig

Farm Swan

Stand for Corn

Farm Pony

Farm Skunk

Rooster

Country Corn

Farm Goat

Farm Hen

MILK

Milk Can

Sheep

Farm Cow

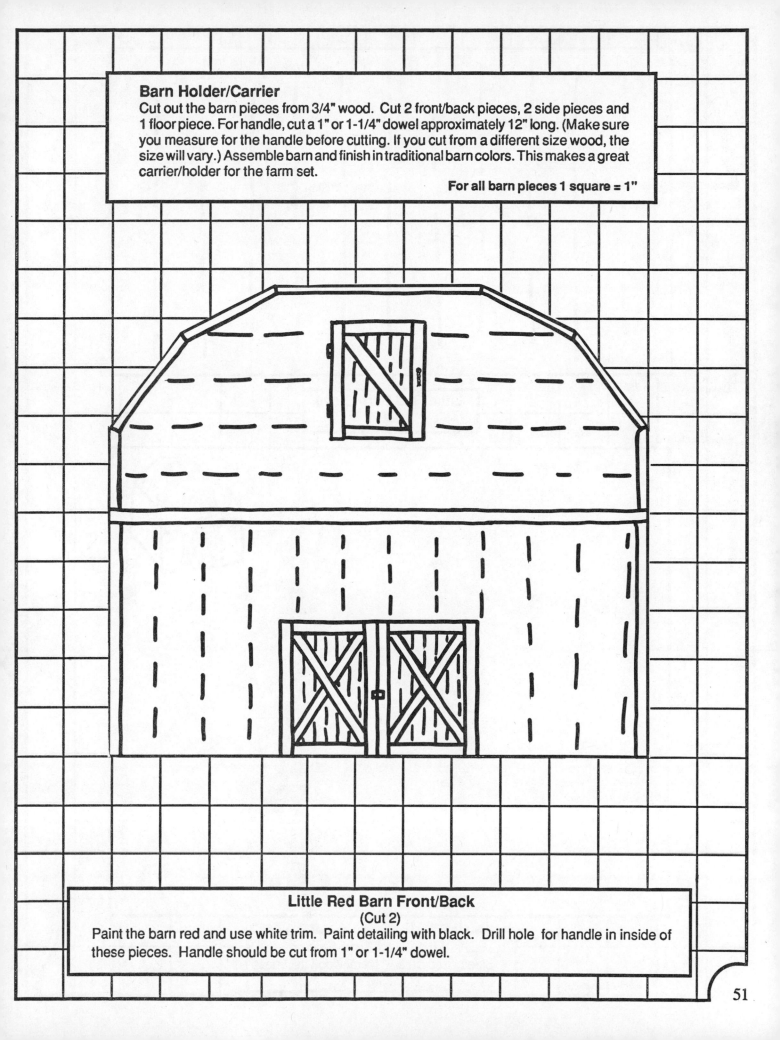

Barn Holder/Carrier

Cut out the barn pieces from 3/4" wood. Cut 2 front/back pieces, 2 side pieces and 1 floor piece. For handle, cut a 1" or 1-1/4" dowel approximately 12" long. (Make sure you measure for the handle before cutting. If you cut from a different size wood, the size will vary.) Assemble barn and finish in traditional barn colors. This makes a great carrier/holder for the farm set.

For all barn pieces 1 square = 1"

Little Red Barn Front/Back
(Cut 2)
Paint the barn red and use white trim. Paint detailing with black. Drill hole for handle in inside of these pieces. Handle should be cut from 1" or 1-1/4" dowel.

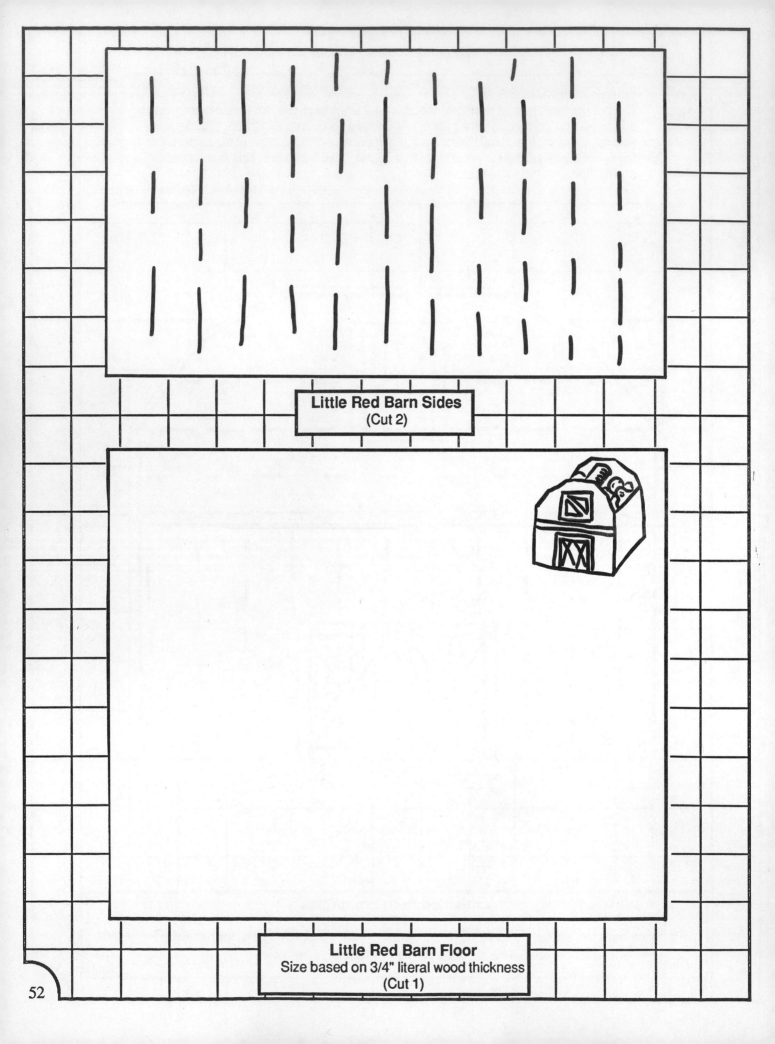

Little Red Barn Sides
(Cut 2)

Little Red Barn Floor
Size based on 3/4" literal wood thickness
(Cut 1)

54

Circus Train

For entire train pattern 1 square = 1"

Make train with as many cars as desired. Cut out Circus animals and performers. They ride in train cars. Kids will be able to use their imagination for endless hours with this play set.Circus Train Directions

All cars (even the engine) are basically the same. Eleven motifs are given for the sides of the standard train cars (see page 58), and a smoke and fire motif is given for the engine. Choose how many cars you will have and cut out 2 side pieces for the engine and each car. Drill two 7/16" holes in each side for axle and wheel assembly.

The engine and cars have the same basic assembly (see standard train car). Cut out 2 side pieces, 2 front/back pieces and 1 floor piece. Attach side pieces to floor piece (floor piece will be placed above the axles). Front/back pieces will fit flush with the side pieces and resemble a box with a raised bottom.

Assemble engine pieces. Attach partial engine roof with small nails and glue. Attach cow catcher to front using catcher support underneath on bottom front of car. Attach engine front motif pieces and glue smoke stack to top.

Paint engine smoke and fire design on side. Choose car motifs and paint sides of cars as desired. Paint remaining cars and wheels in bright colors. Assemble wheels onto each car using dowels for axles. Use glue to secure. Circus Playtime Figures should be stored in cars.

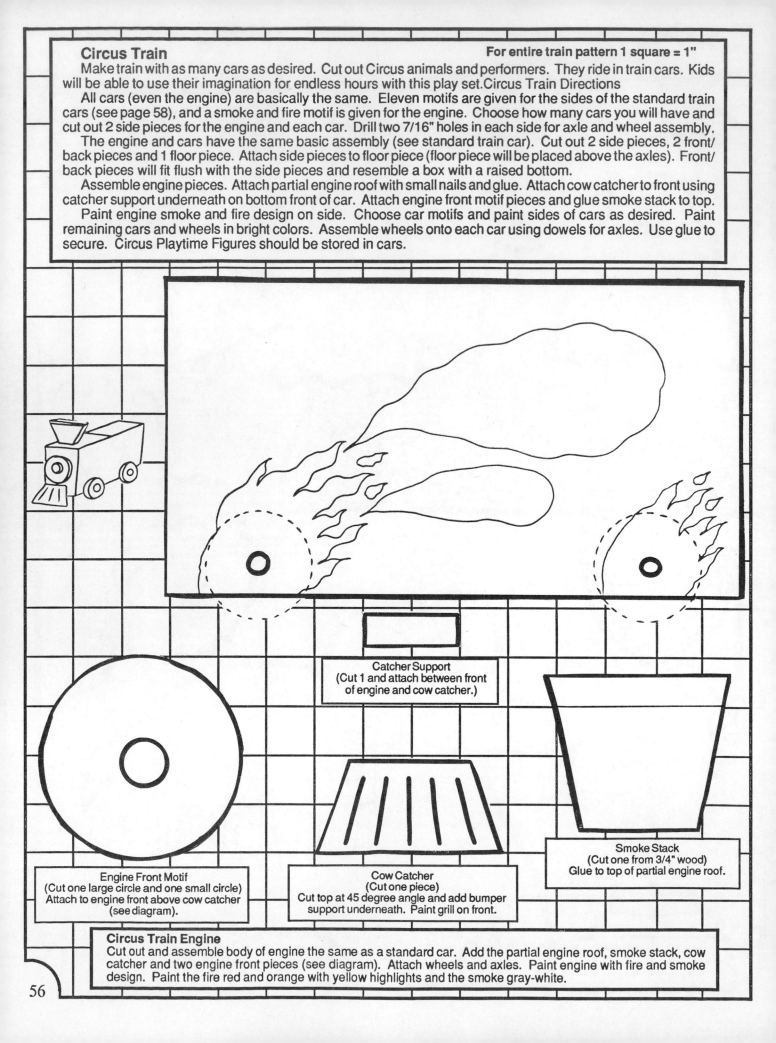

Catcher Support
(Cut 1 and attach between front of engine and cow catcher.)

Smoke Stack
(Cut one from 3/4" wood)
Glue to top of partial engine roof.

Engine Front Motif
(Cut one large circle and one small circle)
Attach to engine front above cow catcher
(see diagram).

Cow Catcher
(Cut one piece)
Cut top at 45 degree angle and add bumper
support underneath. Paint grill on front.

Circus Train Engine

Cut out and assemble body of engine the same as a standard car. Add the partial engine roof, smoke stack, cow catcher and two engine front pieces (see diagram). Attach wheels and axles. Paint engine with fire and smoke design. Paint the fire red and orange with yellow highlights and the smoke gray-white.

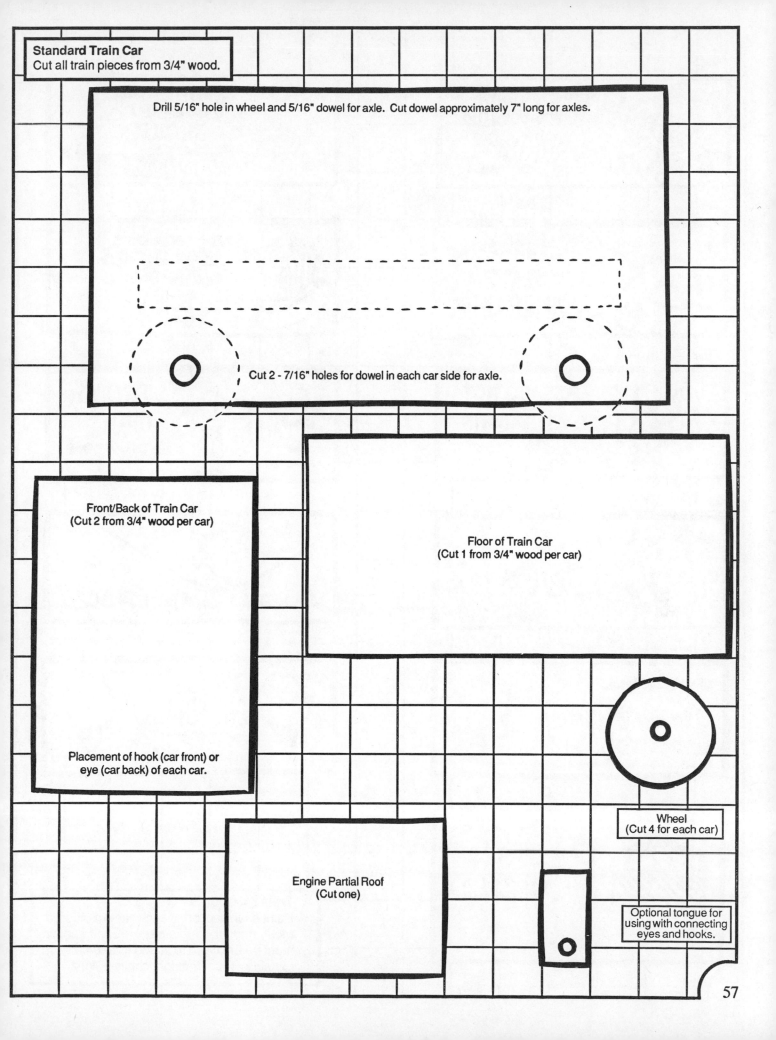

Standard Train Car
Cut all train pieces from 3/4" wood.

Drill 5/16" hole in wheel and 5/16" dowel for axle. Cut dowel approximately 7" long for axles.

Cut 2 - 7/16" holes for dowel in each car side for axle.

Front/Back of Train Car
(Cut 2 from 3/4" wood per car)

Floor of Train Car
(Cut 1 from 3/4" wood per car)

Placement of hook (car front) or
eye (car back) of each car.

Wheel
(Cut 4 for each car)

Engine Partial Roof
(Cut one)

Optional tongue for
using with connecting
eyes and hooks.

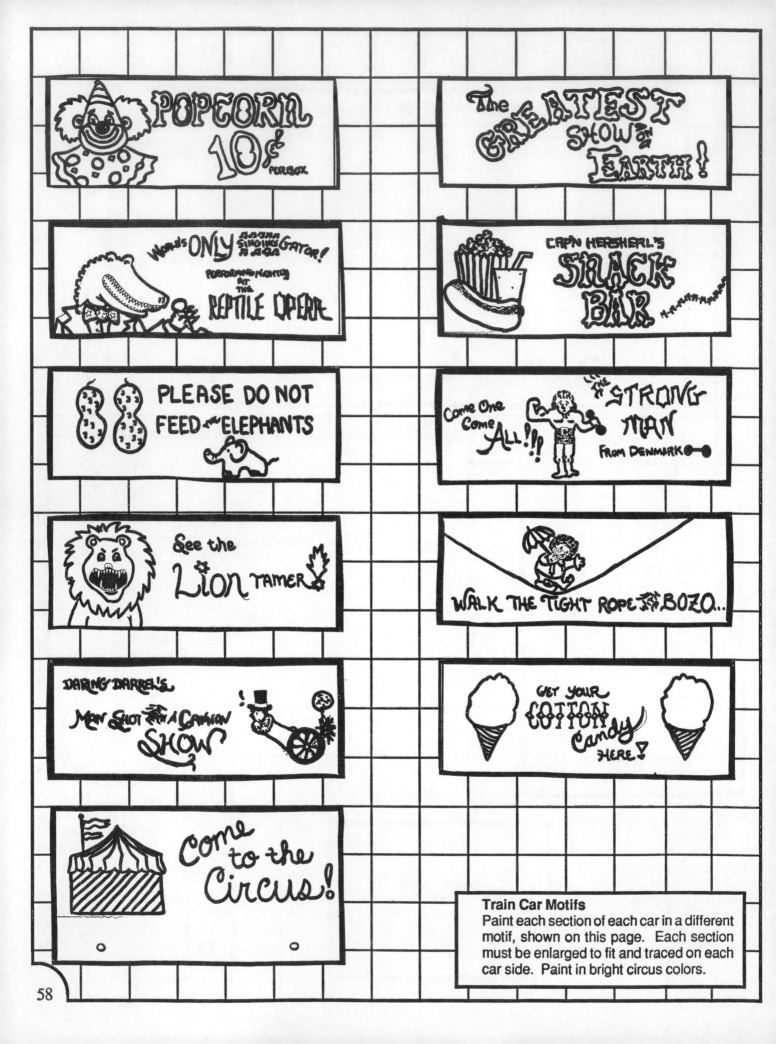

Train Car Motifs
Paint each section of each car in a different motif, shown on this page. Each section must be enlarged to fit and traced on each car side. Paint in bright circus colors.

Animals

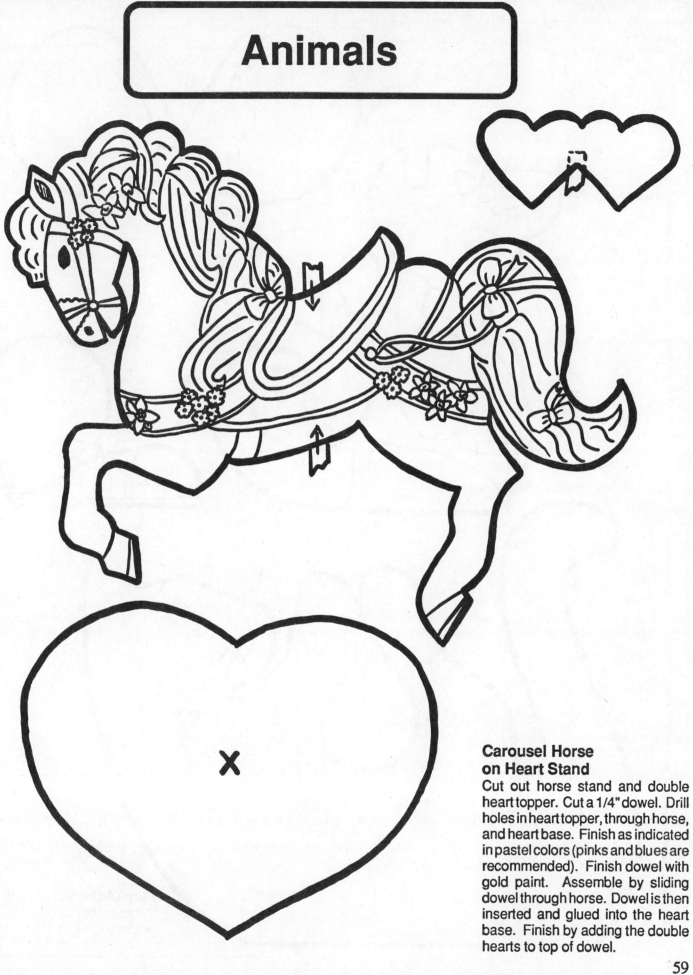

X

**Carousel Horse
on Heart Stand**
Cut out horse stand and double
heart topper. Cut a 1/4" dowel. Drill
holes in heart topper, through horse,
and heart base. Finish as indicated
in pastel colors (pinks and blues are
recommended). Finish dowel with
gold paint. Assemble by sliding
dowel through horse. Dowel is then
inserted and glued into the heart
base. Finish by adding the double
hearts to top of dowel.

3-D Church Mouse

Cut out 1 body and 2 back legs from 1/2" wood. Cut 2 front legs and 1 set of ears from 1/4" wood. Assemble and paint gray with black detailing.

Playful Cat Silhouette

Cut from 3/4" wood. Paint black or white.

Holstein Cow on a Base

Cut cow from 3/4" wood and drill underneath as indicated for dowel. Finish in black and white. Cut a 3/8" dowel the desired length. Cut a 2" x 4" stand and drill a hole in the center for a 3/8" dowel. Paint or stain dowel and base. Assemble using wood glue.

Miss Dancing Bear Mini-Plaque

Mr. Dancing Bear Mini-Plaque

Glue pipe cleaner for cane.

Zoo Menagerie
Cut from 3/4" wood.

63

A Gaggle of Geese
Cut geese from 3/4" wood. These geese should all stand alone. Follow painting directions on first goose.

Plow Horse Stand Up Decoration

Lamb Base

Country Lamb on Base
Cut from 3/4" wood and attach to sheep base

65

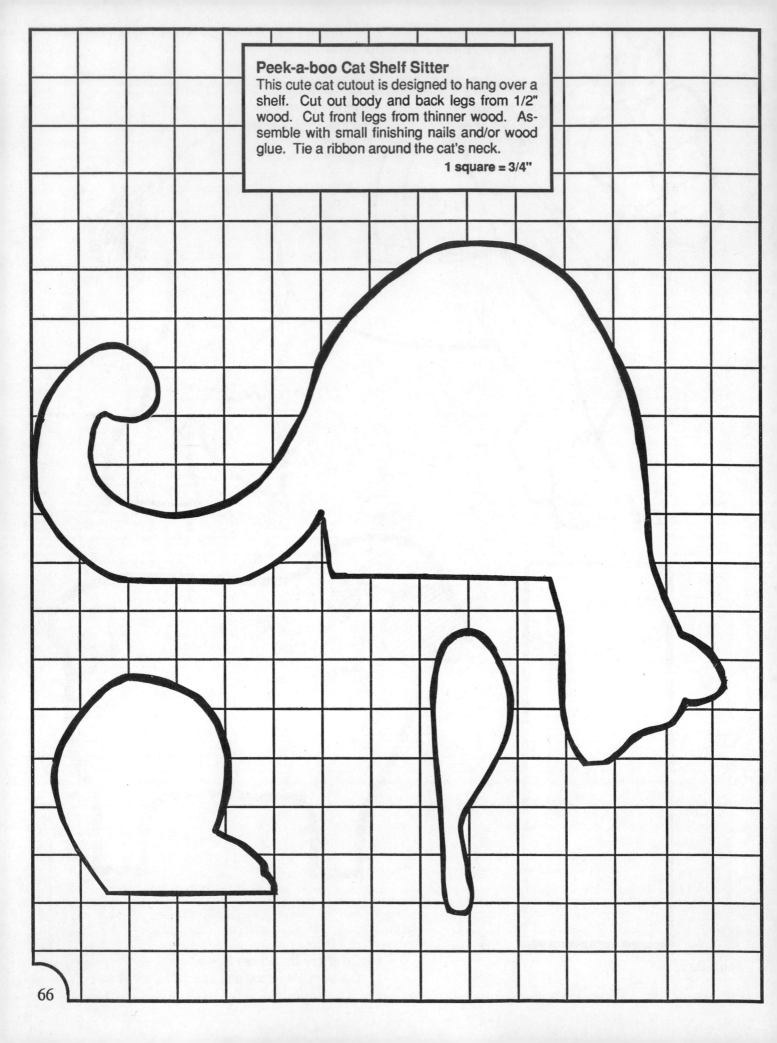

Peek-a-boo Cat Shelf Sitter
This cute cat cutout is designed to hang over a shelf. Cut out body and back legs from 1/2" wood. Cut front legs from thinner wood. Assemble with small finishing nails and/or wood glue. Tie a ribbon around the cat's neck.

1 square = 3/4"

Christmas

Canadian Goose Christmas Greetings Wreath
This wreath is designed especially to decorate a front door. It will last for years and years. Cut wreath out in one piece. Sponge on dark green paint for wreath, paint berries red, goose should be gray and black with white accents. Paint the beak yellow and the ribbon red with black letters. This piece would look good if sponge paints or water-based stains are used. Coat with clear acrylic.

1 square = 1"

Old Fashioned Santa Wall Plaque
Cut out and finish with acrylic paints. Paint name on Santa's bag and attach hanger on back.

The Jones'

Country Christmas Door Sign
Cut out and finish with acrylic paints. Coat with polyurethane. Hang on or beside front door.

1 square = 1"

Yard Soldier   **1 square = 3/4"**
This toy soldier can be used in several ways. Cut out and sit beside the tree for a cut decoration. Enlarge three times, add a base and it will make a nice door sentinel. Enlarge five times for a yard ornament.

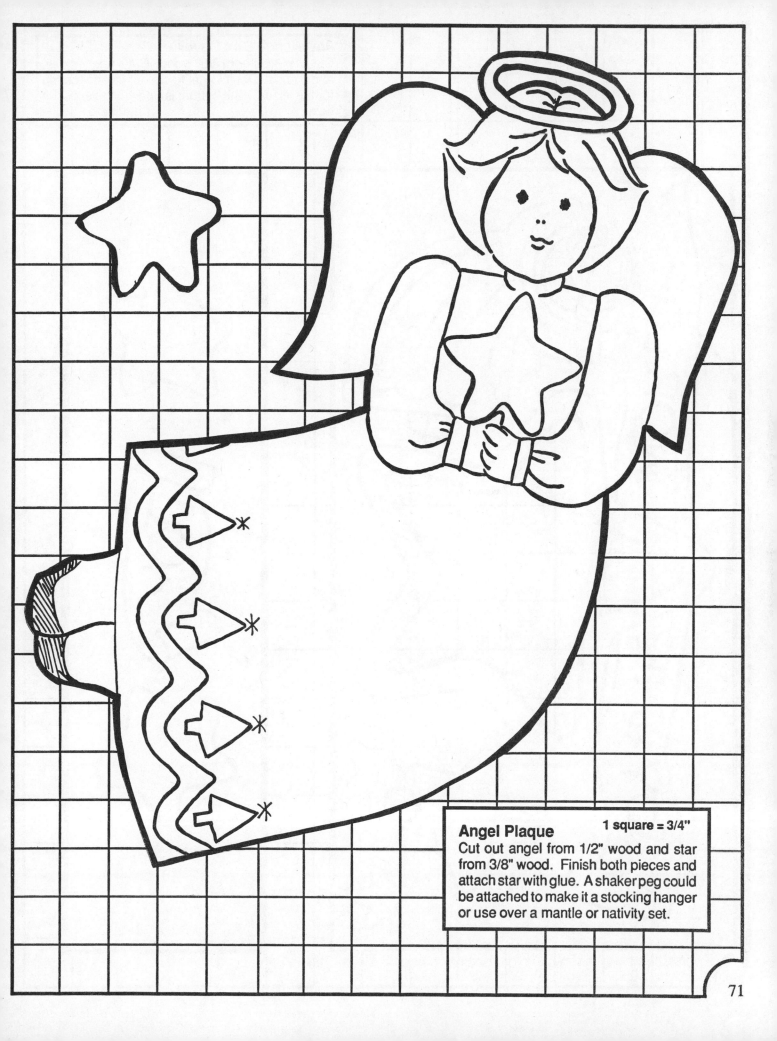

Angel Plaque

1 square = 3/4"

Cut out angel from 1/2" wood and star from 3/8" wood. Finish both pieces and attach star with glue. A shaker peg could be attached to make it a stocking hanger or use over a mantle or nativity set.

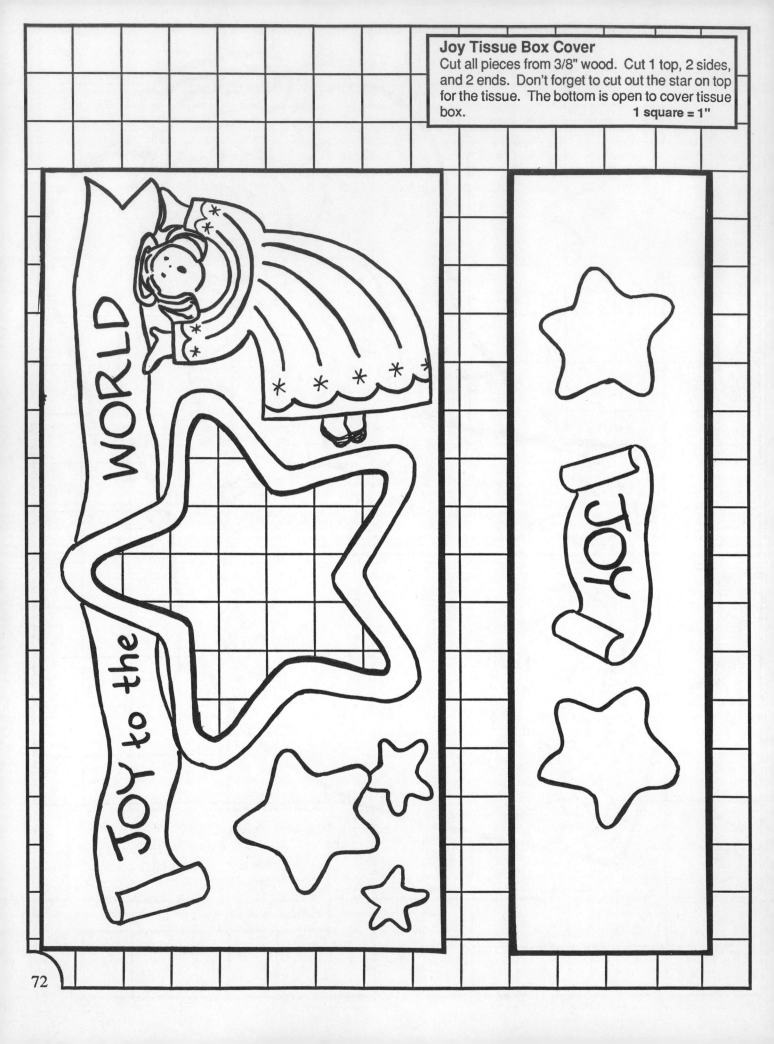

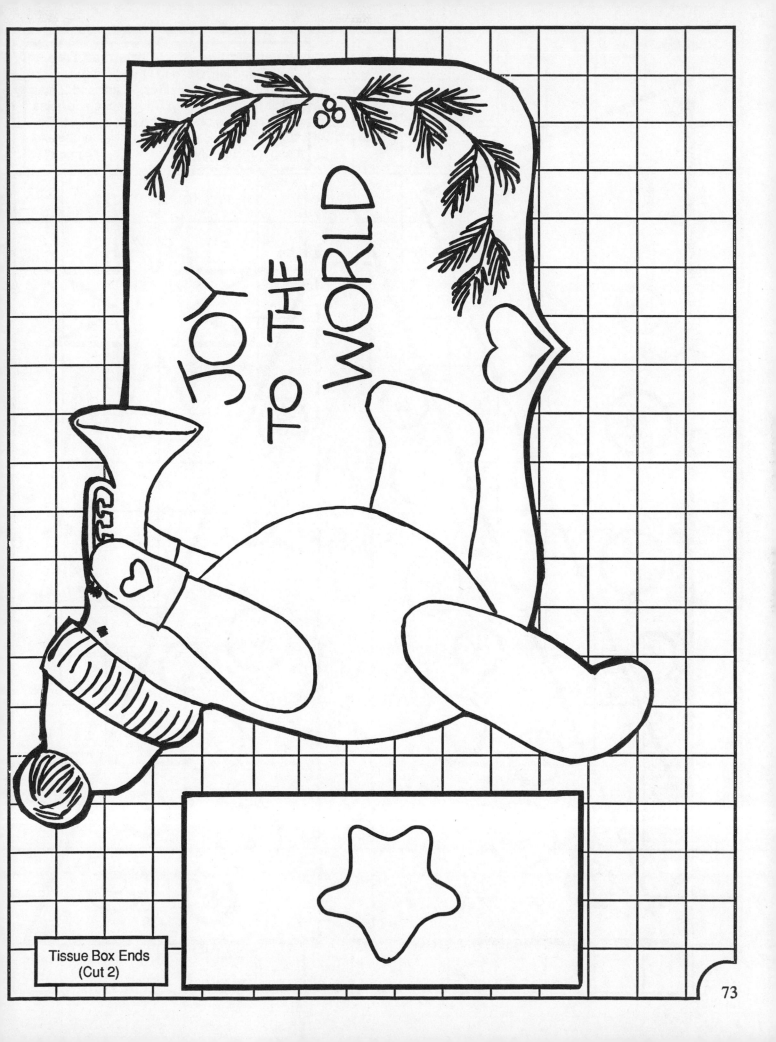

JOY TO THE WORLD

Tissue Box Ends
(Cut 2)

73

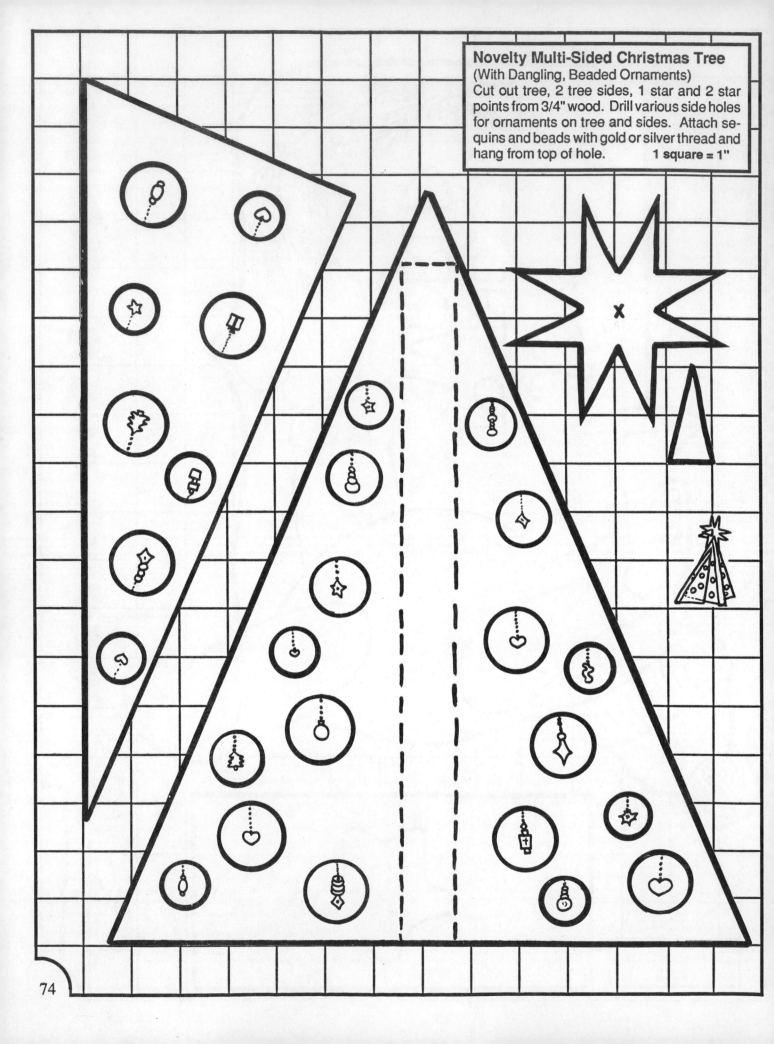

Novelty Multi-Sided Christmas Tree
(With Dangling, Beaded Ornaments)
Cut out tree, 2 tree sides, 1 star and 2 star points from 3/4" wood. Drill various side holes for ornaments on tree and sides. Attach sequins and beads with gold or silver thread and hang from top of hole.   **1 square = 1"**

74

Merry Christmas,
Miss Hill
You're a <u>great</u>
teacher!!

First
Christmas
in
our
New
Home!
1990

**Twelve Days of Christmas
Ornament Set**
Decorate your entire Christmas tree
with this creative Christmas ornament
set. For the first day of Christmas, cut
out one ornament. For the second
day of Christmas, cut out two ornaments. For the third day of Christmas,
cut out three ornaments, etc., etc..

5 GOLD RINGS

76

SWANS "A" SWIMMING.....

Stair-Step Mr. & Mrs. Claus
These easy shelf sitters are very easy to make. Cut out body, lap piece and feet for each figure. Assemble and glue together using assembly diagram. Finish in Christmas colors. Coat with clear acrylic. Sit on shelf or mantel.

1 square = 1 - 1/2"

Mr. Claus
Lap Piece
(Cut 1)

Mrs. Claus
Lap Piece
(Cut 1)

BABY'S FIRST CHRISTMAS!! 1990

OUR FIRST CHRISTMAS TOGETHER 1990

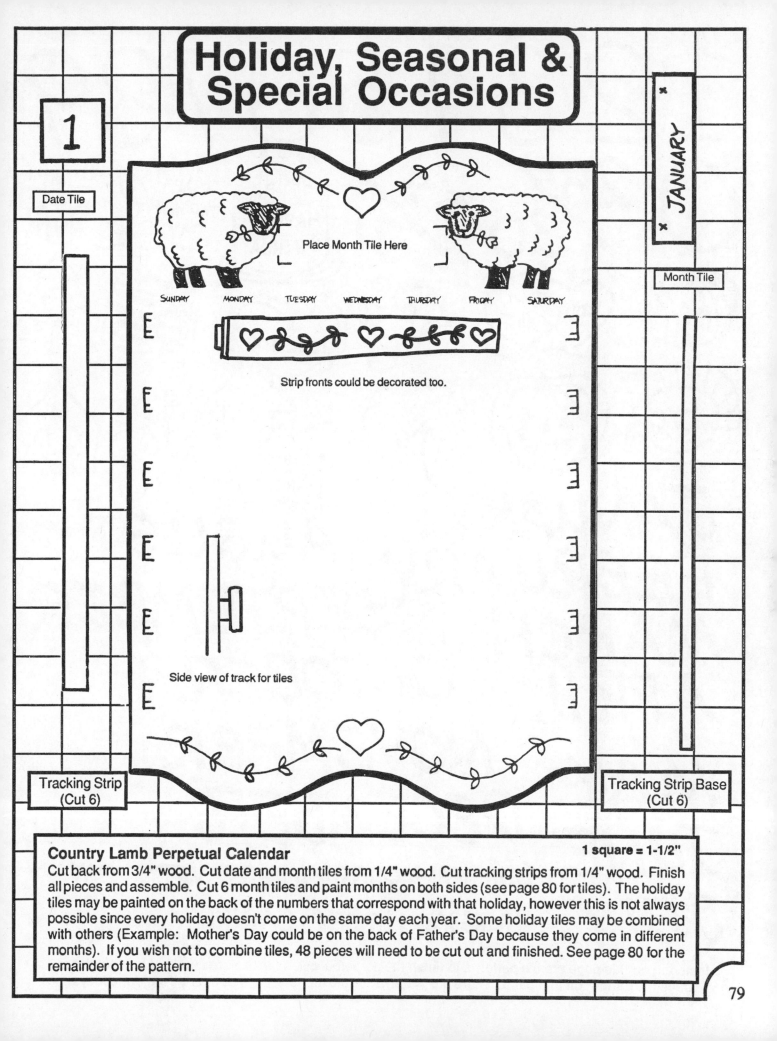

Holiday, Seasonal & Special Occasions

1

Date Tile

JANUARY

Place Month Tile Here

SUNDAY   MONDAY   TUESDAY   WEDNESDAY   THURSDAY   FRIDAY   SATURDAY

Strip fronts could be decorated too.

Side view of track for tiles

Month Tile

Tracking Strip (Cut 6)

Tracking Strip Base (Cut 6)

Country Lamb Perpetual Calendar

1 square = 1-1/2"

Cut back from 3/4" wood. Cut date and month tiles from 1/4" wood. Cut tracking strips from 1/4" wood. Finish all pieces and assemble. Cut 6 month tiles and paint months on both sides (see page 80 for tiles). The holiday tiles may be painted on the back of the numbers that correspond with that holiday, however this is not always possible since every holiday doesn't come on the same day each year. Some holiday tiles may be combined with others (Example: Mother's Day could be on the back of Father's Day because they come in different months). If you wish not to combine tiles, 48 pieces will need to be cut out and finished. See page 80 for the remainder of the pattern.

1 2 3 4 5 6 7 8 9 0 23/30 24/31

HAPPY BIRTHDAY

HAPPY MOTHERS DAY

HE IS ALIVE

John Alice

PAD'S DAY!

I LOVE YOU

SCHOOL

JANUARY
FEBRUARY
MARCH
APRIL
MAY
JUNE
JULY
AUGUST
SEPTEMBER
OCTOBER
NOVEMBER
DECEMBER

SUNDAY MONDAY TUESDAY WEDNESDAY

THURSDAY FRIDAY SATURDAY

Included on this page are the patterns to finish the perpetual calendar. Enlarge and cut out the pieces,
trace the pattern on and paint. There are patterns for the months, days and for all major holidays.

End of the Rainbow/St. Patrick's Day Mobile

Cut out one base and as many hanging pieces as you desire. Drill small holes to hang figures. Hang with fishing line. Attach a string to hang where indicated by an x.

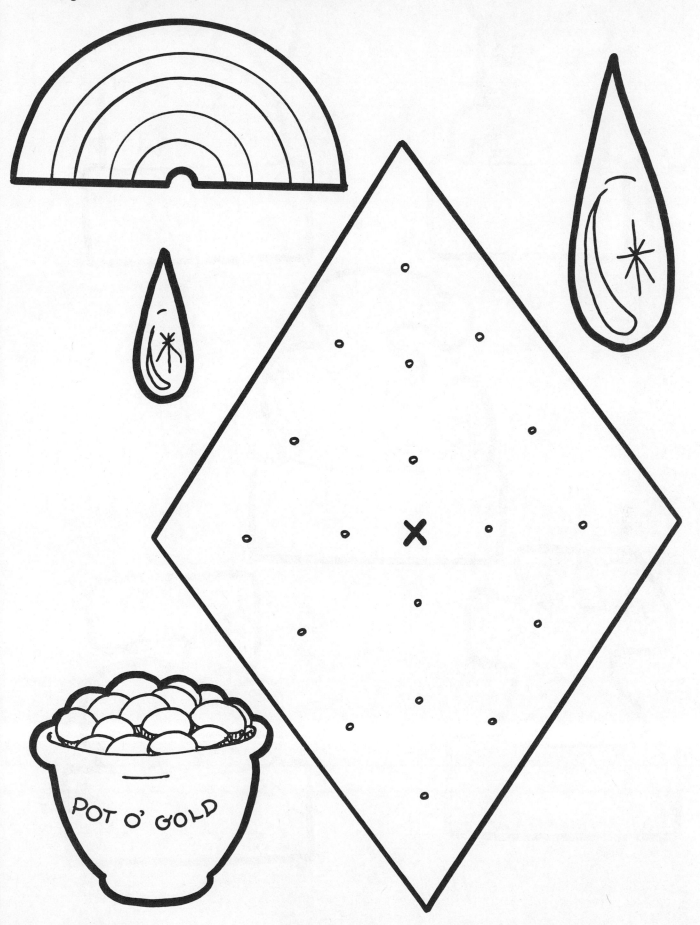

X

POT O' GOLD

Birthday Candle Holders

Make 2 complete sets of candle holders to be ready to celebrate any birthday from 1-100. Just insert a candle and place it on top of an iced cake and you have an instant birthday cake!

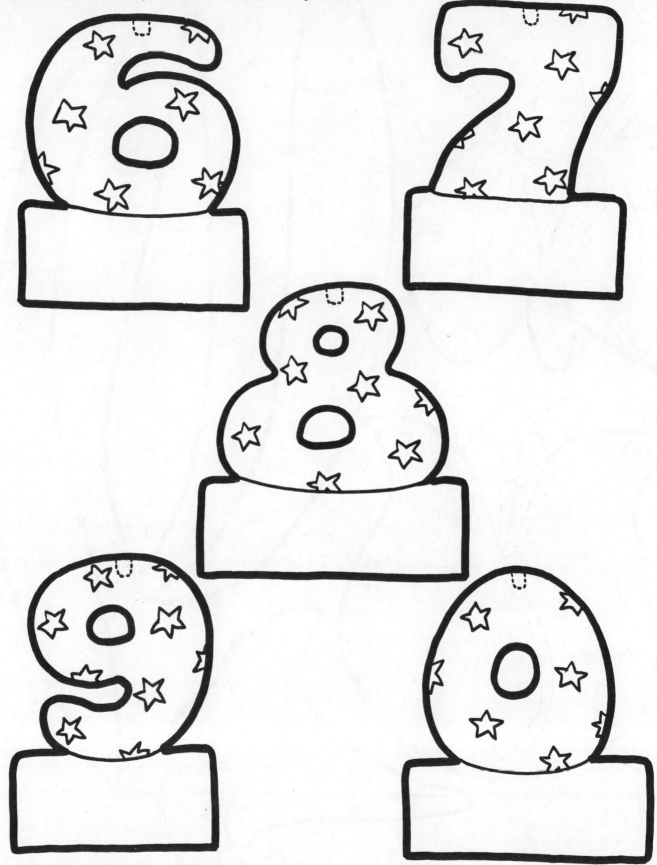

Flowers and Planter

An assortment of flowers are given to be used either with the planter or in a regular flower arrangement. If using with planter: Cut out 1 or 2 flowers, attach 3/8" dowel to flower head. This will make a stem. Drill holes to planter. Attach leaves. For an arrangement: Cut out as many flowers as needed for arrangement and attach flower head to dowel. Finish. Cut out desired leaves, attach to dowel, and paint green. Place styrofoam base in pot or basket, insert flowers and leaves into basket and fill in with baby's breath or statice.

85

Easter Rabbit on Stand

Cut from 3/4" wood. Cut 2 arms. Cut 4" x 4" square for stand. Drill rabbit and stand for 3/8" dowel. Finish both sides, glue on arms and attach to stand, using dowel.

Canadian Goose

Cut from 3/4" wood. Cut 2 wings. Cut 4" x 4" square for stand. Drill goose and stand for 3/8" dowel. Finish both sides, glue on wings and attach to stand, using dowel.

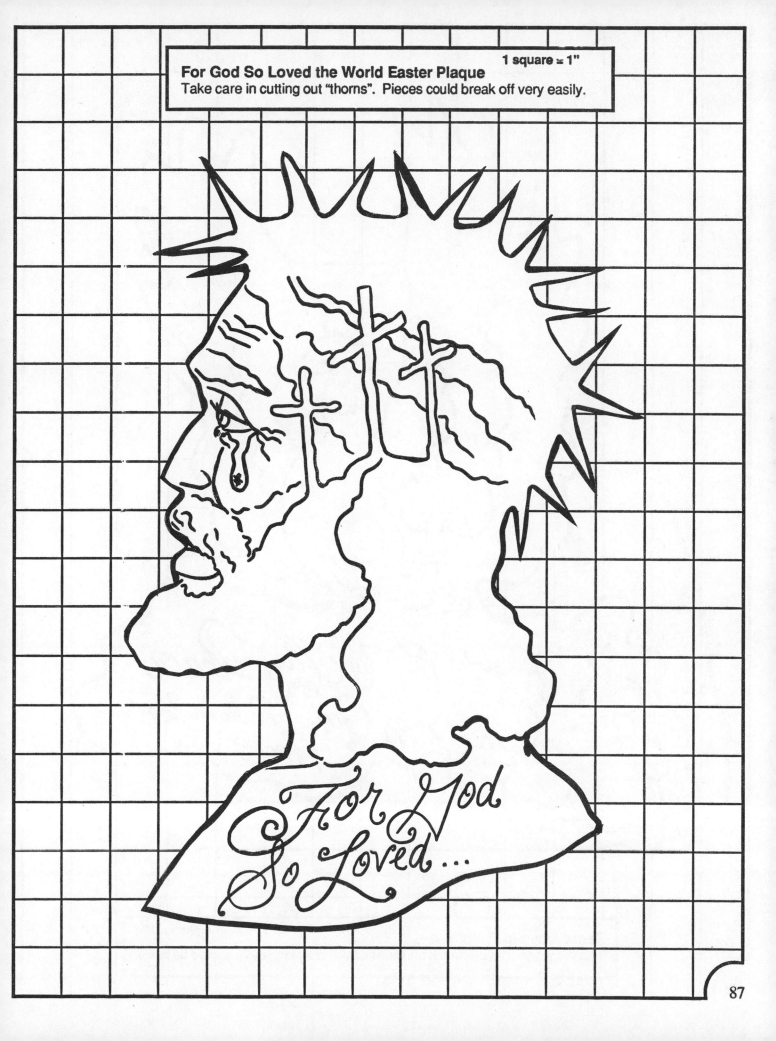

For God So Loved the World Easter Plaque
Take care in cutting out "thorns". Pieces could break off very easily.

1 square = 1"

For God So Loved...

Peace Dove in Flight

This plaque should be cut out and finished with acrylics. Dove should be white.

1 square = 1"

May The Peace of God Rule in Your Heart

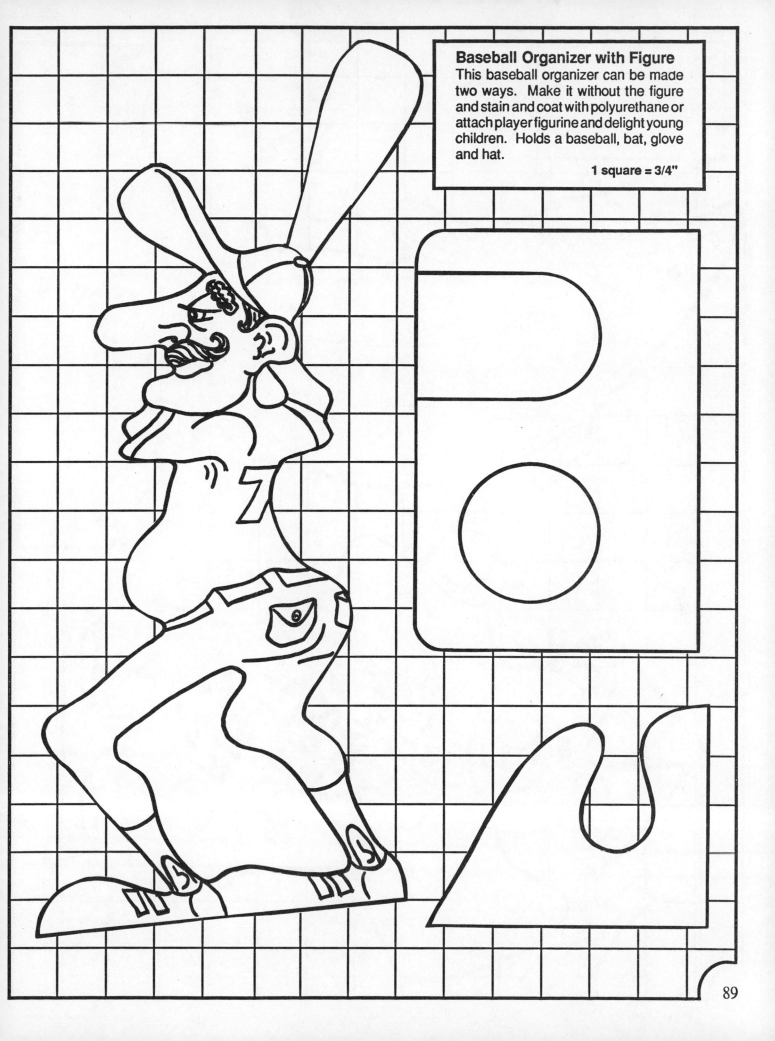

Baseball Organizer with Figure
This baseball organizer can be made two ways. Make it without the figure and stain and coat with polyurethane or attach player figurine and delight young children. Holds a baseball, bat, glove and hat.

1 square = 3/4"

Fish Plaque
Cut out this fish plaque for hanging fishing gear. Attach hooks where indicated by X's

1 square = 3/4"

90

**Graduation Figures/
Centerpieces**
Cut out from 3/4" wood. Paint as
indicated. Use these pieces for
table centerpieces or decorations
at graduation parties.

Uncle Sam
Independence Day Shelf/Figure

1 square = 3/4"

Cut from 3/4" stock. Finish, attach shelves as shown and use for Americana miniature collectables.

If enlarged 6 times, this will become a life-sized holiday yard ornament. Cut from exterior plywood. Paint as indicated and attach stakes to back and insert into ground.

Shelf

Country School Girl Plaque
1 square = 3/4"

92

Door Harps

the
MEYERS

For All Door Harps — 1 square = 3/4"

Door Harp Instructions

Cut out and finish as shown. This door harp does not need a back. It would be best to purchase a door harp assemby from a hardware store, craft store, or order from a wood worker's supply mail order catalog.

For do-it-yourselfers — the quality will not necessarily be the same but you may assemble by attaching eye hooks to string wire on. You could also purchase guitar strings and posts to mount strings. Purchase wooden balls from a hardware store. String balls on fishing line. Attach by cutting two thin wooden bars at top of harp assembly and glue together, clamping fishing line between two pieces of wood. Make sure each ball strikes wires to make a musical sound. Hang on door so that when the door is opened and closed, the harp is played.

93

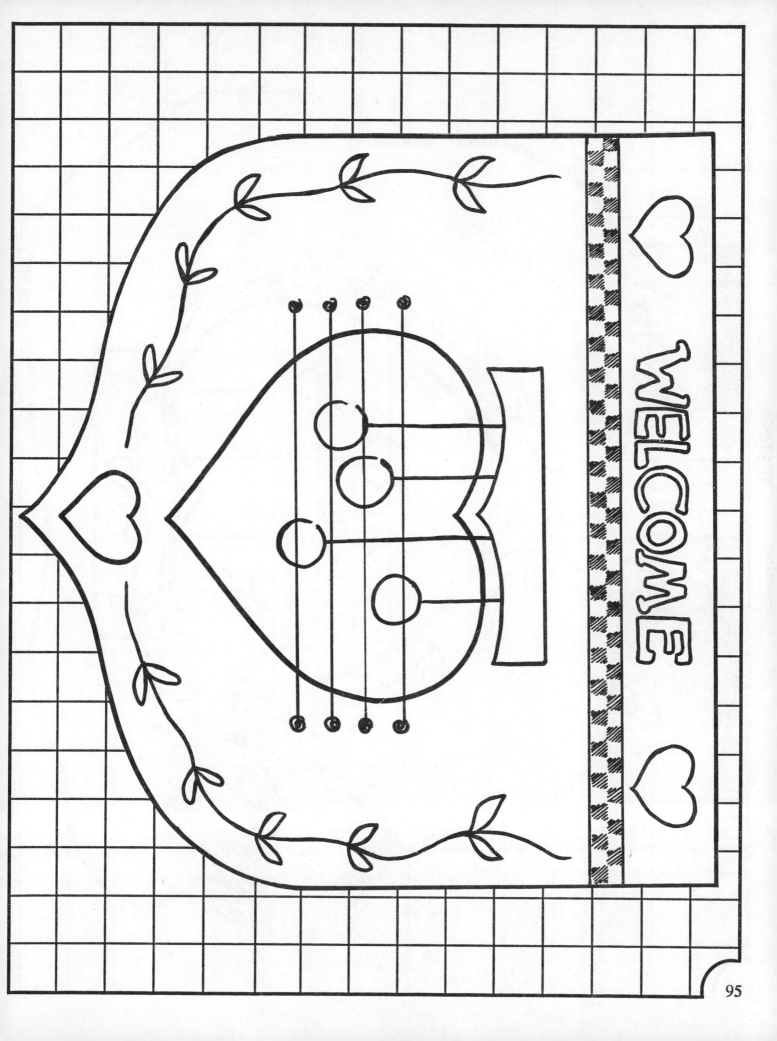

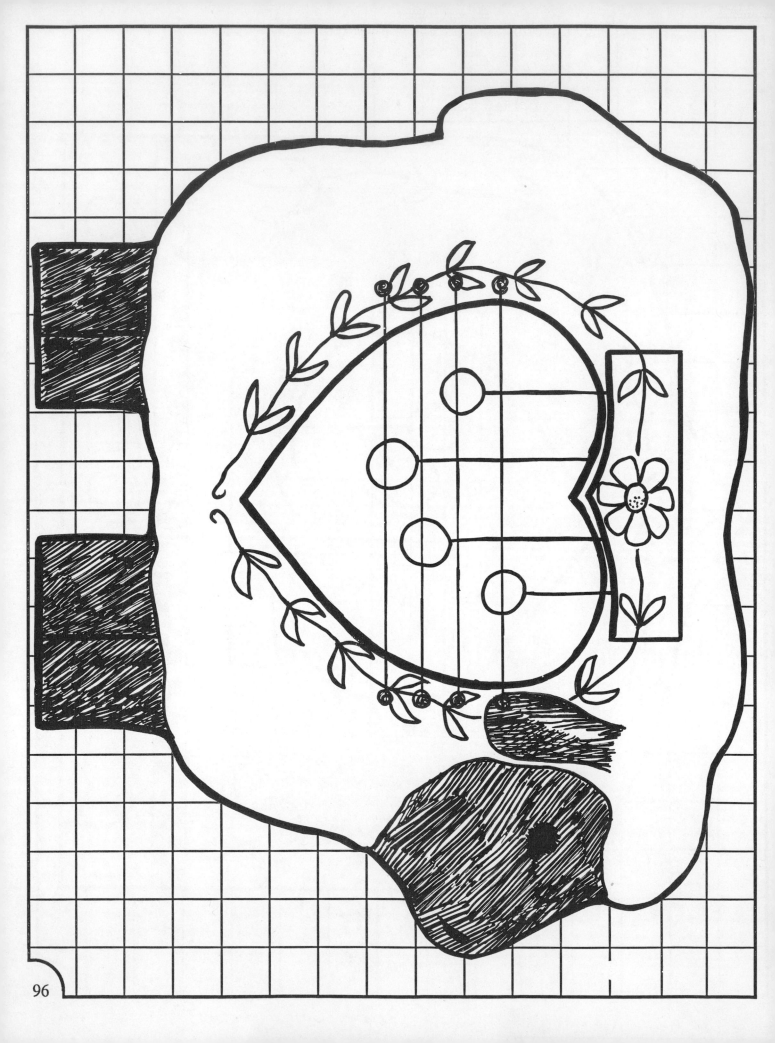

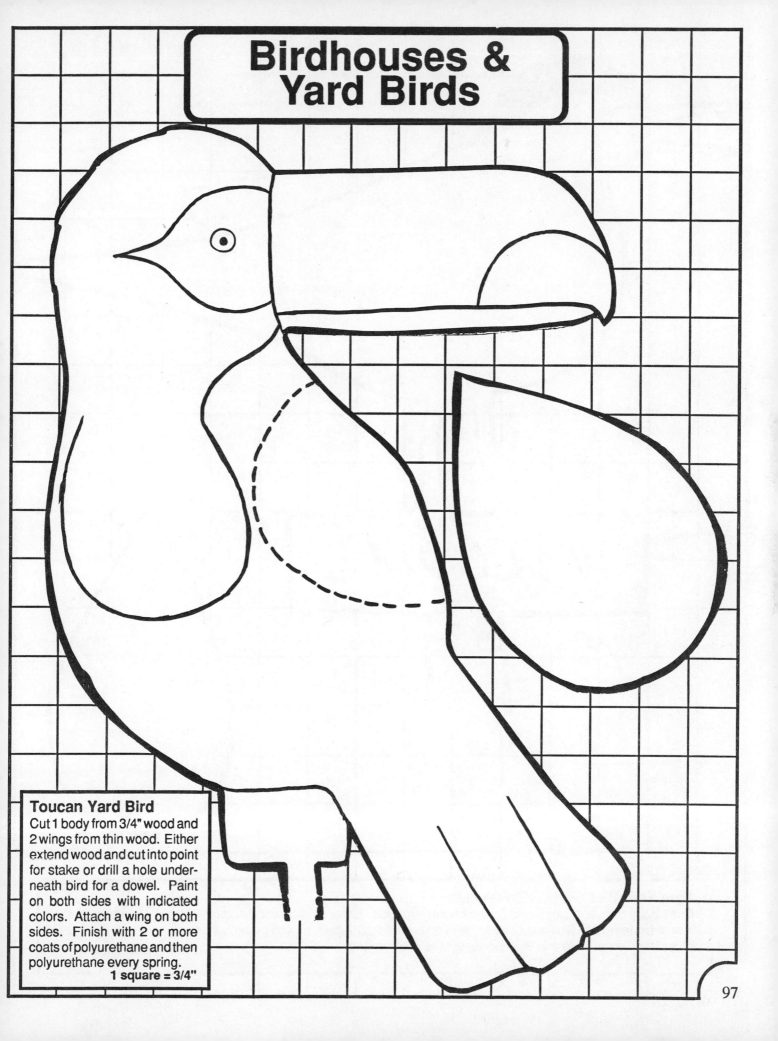

Birdhouses & Yard Birds

Toucan Yard Bird
Cut 1 body from 3/4" wood and 2 wings from thin wood. Either extend wood and cut into point for stake or drill a hole underneath bird for a dowel. Paint on both sides with indicated colors. Attach a wing on both sides. Finish with 2 or more coats of polyurethane and then polyurethane every spring.
1 square = 3/4"

WELCOME

Tern Yard Bird with Welcome Plate
Cut 1 body from 3/4" wood and 2 wings from thin wood. Either extend wood and cut into point for stake or drill a hole underneath bird for a dowel. Paint on both sides. Attach a wing on both sides. Finish with 2 or more coats of polyurethane and then polyurethane every spring.

1 square = 3/4"

Heart and Home Birdhouse Duplex

1 square = 1-1/2"

Cut 2 front pieces, 2 side pieces, 2 roof pieces and 2 bottom pieces. Cut out holes for birds as shown (black circles) and drill holes for 3/8" dowel in front piece (as indicated by x's) for bird perch. Assemble front, back and sides. Attach one of the bottom pieces in the middle (as indicated by the dashed line) and at the bottom of the birdhouse. Assemble the roof. Paint on designs as indicated. Finish outside with polyurethane. Do not paint inside. Glue dowel in hole for perch.

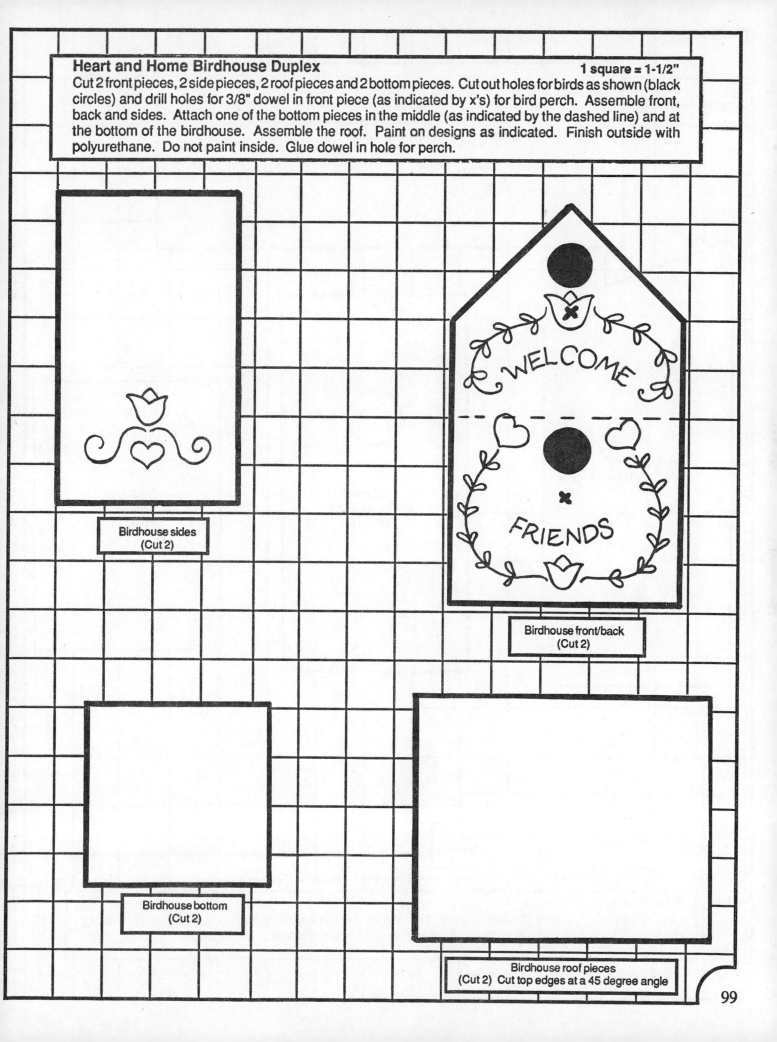

Birdhouse sides
(Cut 2)

WELCOME

FRIENDS

Birdhouse front/back
(Cut 2)

Birdhouse bottom
(Cut 2)

Birdhouse roof pieces
(Cut 2) Cut top edges at a 45 degree angle

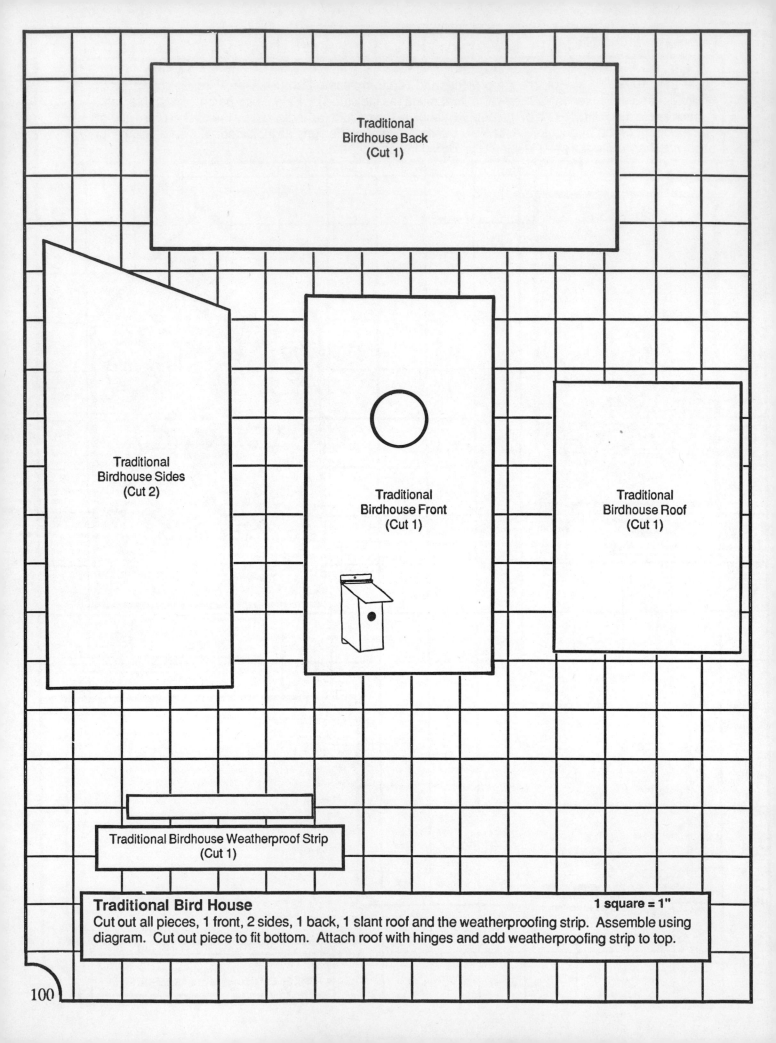

Traditional
Birdhouse Back
(Cut 1)

Traditional
Birdhouse Sides
(Cut 2)

Traditional
Birdhouse Front
(Cut 1)

Traditional
Birdhouse Roof
(Cut 1)

Traditional Birdhouse Weatherproof Strip
(Cut 1)

Traditional Bird House   1 square = 1"
Cut out all pieces, 1 front, 2 sides, 1 back, 1 slant roof and the weatherproofing strip. Assemble using
diagram. Cut out piece to fit bottom. Attach roof with hinges and add weatherproofing strip to top.

Weather Vanes, Whirligigs & Yard Ornaments

For All Weather Vane Patterns — 1 square = 1"

These weather vane designs and yard ornaments are meant to be decorative. Adjustments to the weather vane pattern will need to be made before the weather vane will turn with the wind. All outdoor pieces need to be coated several times with polyurethane after painting to preserve the painting details and prevent weathering. The entire piece will need coating every year for continued protection.

Deluxe Weather Vane Stand
Instructions:
1. Choose Motif
2. Combine pattern with stand
3. Cut stand and motif out in 1 piece

Always use treated wood for outdoor pieces. Coat 2 or 3 times with polyurethane.

For a weather vane that moves with the wind: Cut weather vane into 2 pieces (as shown). Drill a hole in the bottom piece and insert a dowel in the top piece, securing with glue. The dowel will allow the arrow to rotate with the wind. Another option is to check your hardware supply store for hardware to allow pieces to rotate (1 option is PVC if the correct sizes are in stock). The motif and arrow will move with the wind. The North and South directional piece should remain stationary.

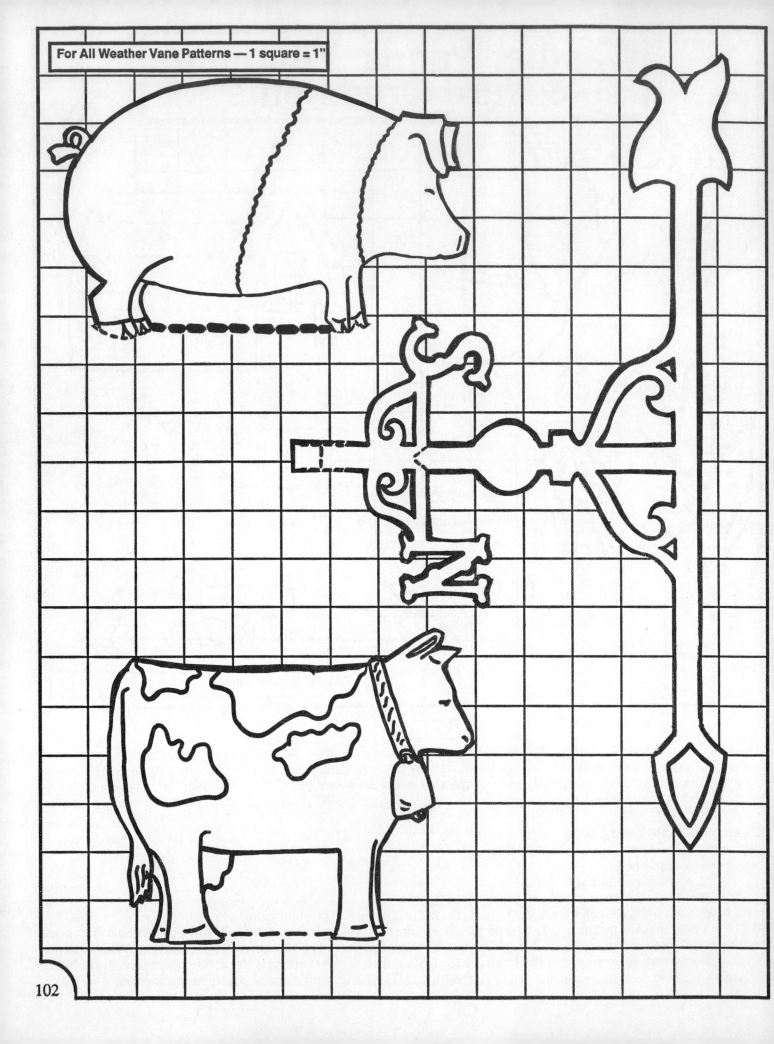

For All Weather Vane Patterns — 1 square = 1"

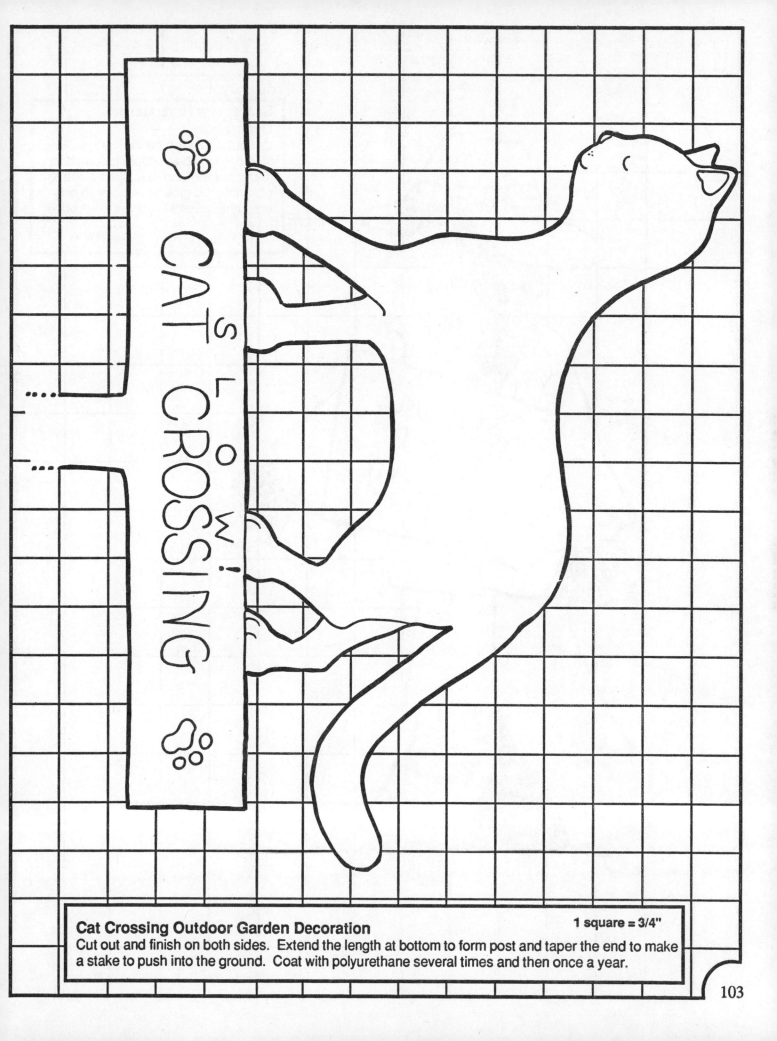

Cat Crossing Outdoor Garden Decoration
Cut out and finish on both sides. Extend the length at bottom to form post and taper the end to make a stake to push into the ground. Coat with polyurethane several times and then once a year.

1 square = 3/4"

CAT CROSSING SLOW!

Scarecrow Herb Garden Decoration

Cut out and finish on both sides. Extend the length at bottom to form post and taper the end to make a stake to push into the ground. Coat with polyurethane several times and then once a year.

1 square - 1"

WELCOME TO MY GARDEN!

Whirligig Assembly Instructions

Use 3/4" wood for body of Whirligig, 3/4" wood for block and blade base. Use 1/8" wood for blades. Cut 2 blade bases, 2 blocks and 4 blades for each Whirligig. (Arrows on blade patterns indicate which end goes into block.) Attach a blade base to each side of Whirligig where indicated by an x. Two 2" screws and 4 metal washers will also be needed for each assembly. Glue blades into wooden blocks. Attach to blade base with metal washers and screw in following order — metal washer, block, metal washer. Drill hole underneath Whirligig and insert wooden (or metal) dowel. Drill hole for dowel into outside post and insert Whirligig on dowel into hole. This assembly will cause the Whirligig to have some wind movement.

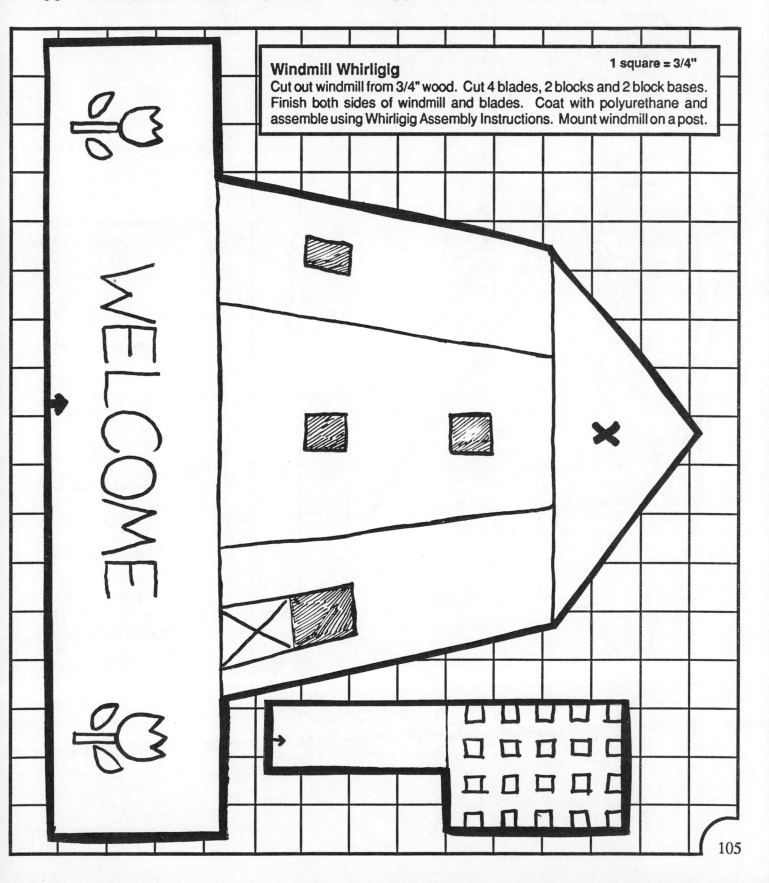

Windmill Whirligig

1 square = 3/4"

Cut out windmill from 3/4" wood. Cut 4 blades, 2 blocks and 2 block bases. Finish both sides of windmill and blades. Coat with polyurethane and assemble using Whirligig Assembly Instructions. Mount windmill on a post.

WELCOME

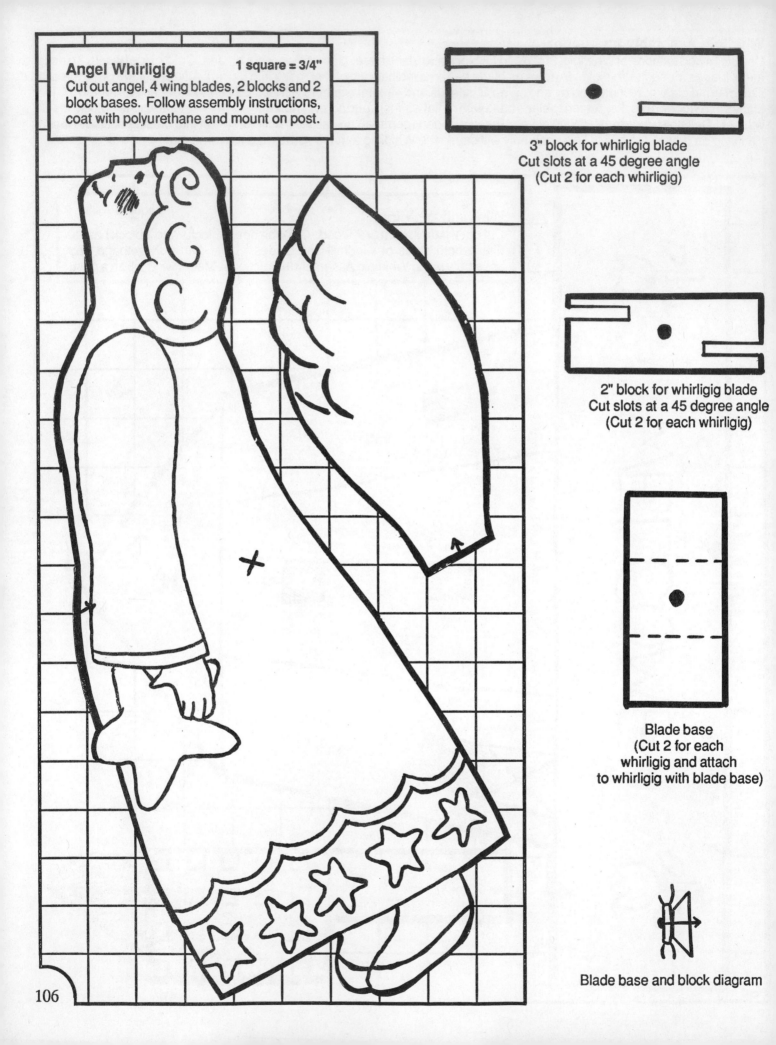

Angel Whirligig
Cut out angel, 4 wing blades, 2 blocks and 2 block bases. Follow assembly instructions, coat with polyurethane and mount on post.

1 square = 3/4"

3" block for whirligig blade
Cut slots at a 45 degree angle
(Cut 2 for each whirligig)

2" block for whirligig blade
Cut slots at a 45 degree angle
(Cut 2 for each whirligig)

Blade base
(Cut 2 for each
whirligig and attach
to whirligig with blade base)

Blade base and block diagram

Washwoman Whirligig

1 square = 3/4"

Cut out washwoman, wash basket, 4 arm blades, 2 blocks and 2 block bases. Use Assembly instructions. Coat with polyurethane and mount on post.

Cat Whirligig

1 square = 3/4"

Cut out cat, 4 arm blades, 2 blocks and 2 block bases. Follow assembly instructions. coat with polyurethane and mount on post.

Bear Whirligig

1 square = 3/4"

Cut out bear, 4 arm blades, 2 blocks and 2 block bases. Follow assembly instructions, coat with polyurethane and mount on post.

Kitchen Accessories

Holstein Cow Paper Towel Holder

1 square = 3/4"

Cut 1 cow and 1 base from 3/4" wood. Cut legs separately from thin wood. Cut a 1" dowel 13 inches long to hold towel. Drill hole for dowel in base and attach dowel to base using wood glue. Attach cow to base as indicated by diagram, using wood screws. The legs should be attached with wood glue. Drill a small hole in the cow as shown to insert a knotted and frayed tail made from heavy twine, as shown. Paint white with black spots. Accent with colors to match your decor.

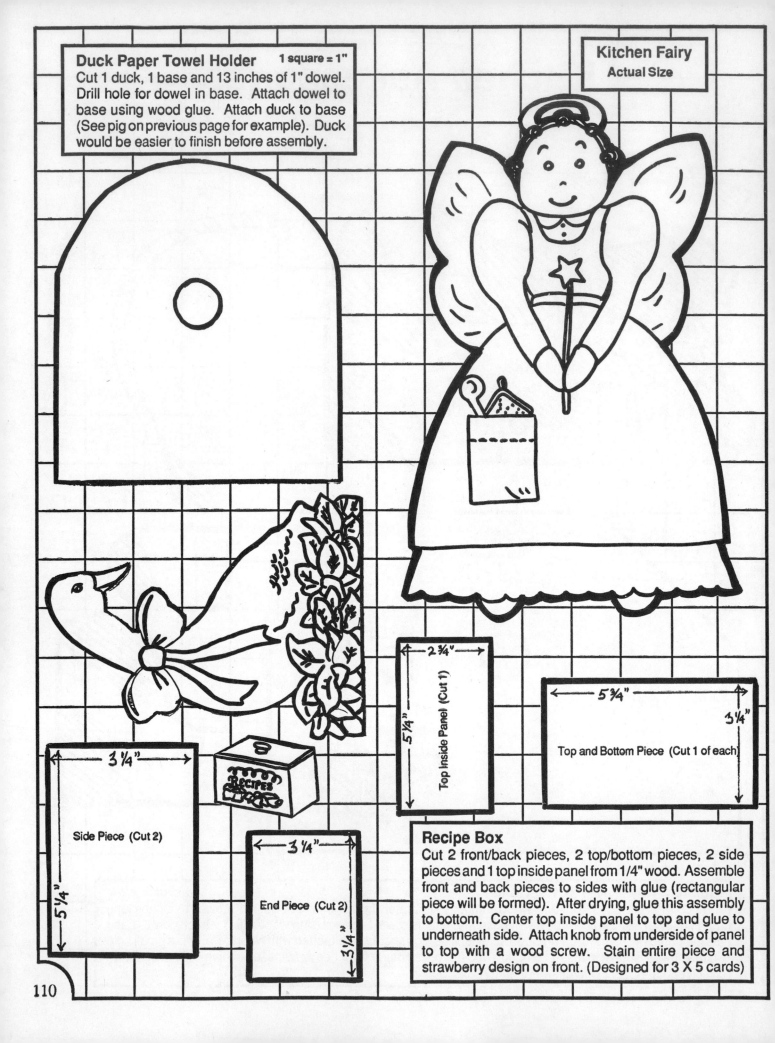

Duck Paper Towel Holder 1 square = 1"

Cut 1 duck, 1 base and 13 inches of 1" dowel.
Drill hole for dowel in base. Attach dowel to
base using wood glue. Attach duck to base
(See pig on previous page for example). Duck
would be easier to finish before assembly.

Kitchen Fairy
Actual Size

Top Inside Panel (Cut 1)
2¾"
5¼"

Top and Bottom Piece (Cut 1 of each)
5¾"
3¼"

Side Piece (Cut 2)
3¼"
5¼"

End Piece (Cut 2)
3¼"
3¼"

RECIPES

Recipe Box

Cut 2 front/back pieces, 2 top/bottom pieces, 2 side
pieces and 1 top inside panel from 1/4" wood. Assemble
front and back pieces to sides with glue (rectangular
piece will be formed). After drying, glue this assembly
to bottom. Center top inside panel to top and glue to
underneath side. Attach knob from underside of panel
to top with a wood screw. Stain entire piece and
strawberry design on front. (Designed for 3 X 5 cards)

Kitchen Set

This complete kitchen set was designed to be cut out and stained, coated with polyurethane and used in the kitchen. The pineapples should be cut out (this would be an inside cut), however if you prefer, the pineapples could be cut separately, finished and glued on. Another motif (such as a duck or a pig) could also be cut separately and attached in place of the pineapple.

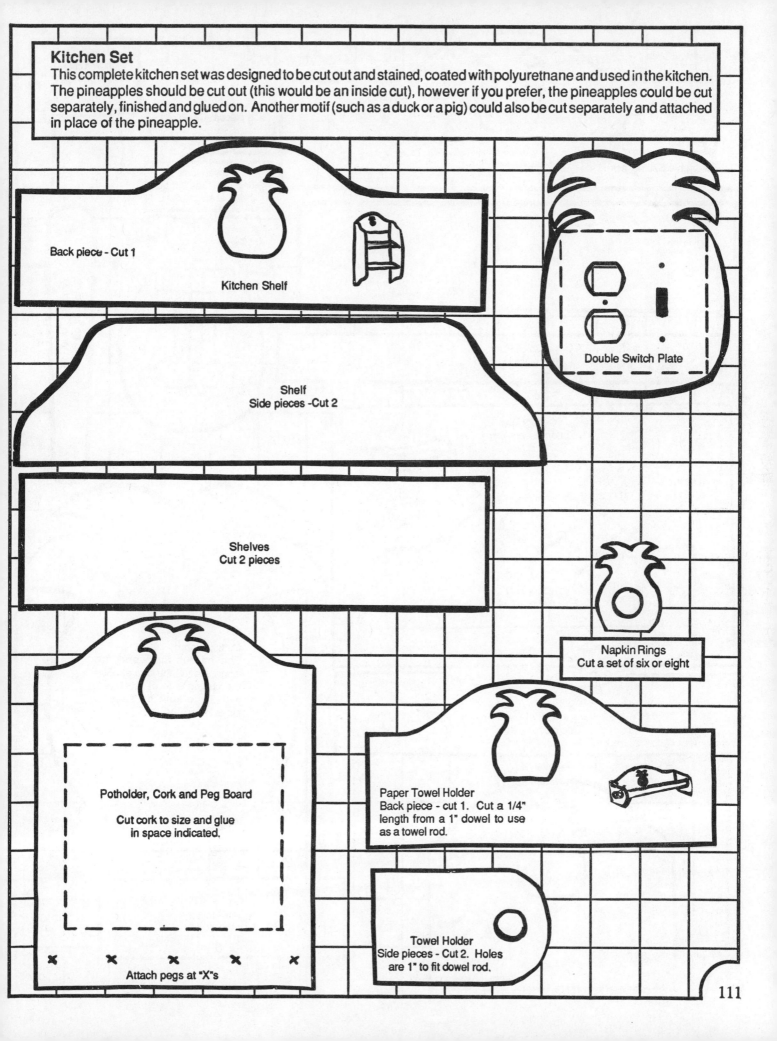

Back piece - Cut 1

Kitchen Shelf

Shelf
Side pieces -Cut 2

Double Switch Plate

Shelves
Cut 2 pieces

Napkin Rings
Cut a set of six or eight

Potholder, Cork and Peg Board

Cut cork to size and glue
in space indicated.

Paper Towel Holder
Back piece - cut 1. Cut a 1/4"
length from a 1" dowel to use
as a towel rod.

Attach pegs at "X"s

Towel Holder
Side pieces - Cut 2. Holes
are 1" to fit dowel rod.

111

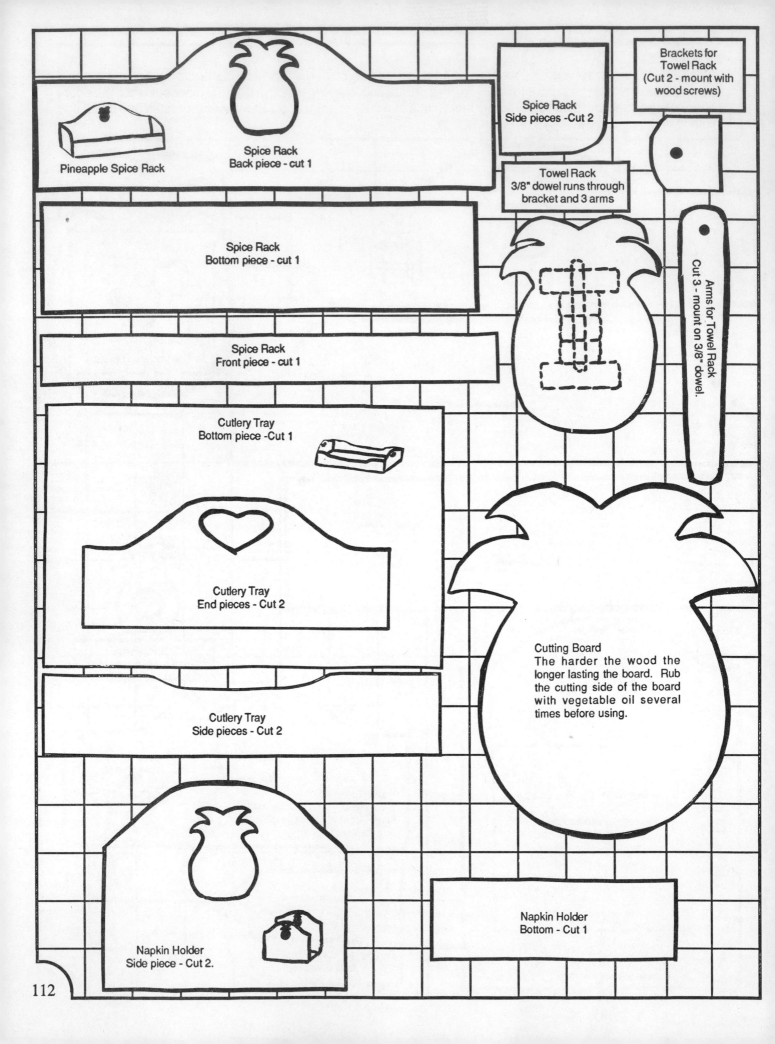

Pineapple Spice Rack

Spice Rack
Back piece - cut 1

Spice Rack
Side pieces - Cut 2

Brackets for
Towel Rack
(Cut 2 - mount with
wood screws)

Spice Rack
Bottom piece - cut 1

Towel Rack
3/8" dowel runs through
bracket and 3 arms

Arms for Towel Rack
Cut 3 - mount on 3/8" dowel.

Spice Rack
Front piece - cut 1

Cutlery Tray
Bottom piece - Cut 1

Cutlery Tray
End pieces - Cut 2

Cutting Board
The harder the wood the
longer lasting the board. Rub
the cutting side of the board
with vegetable oil several
times before using.

Cutlery Tray
Side pieces - Cut 2

Napkin Holder
Side piece - Cut 2.

Napkin Holder
Bottom - Cut 1

112

Bathroom Accessories

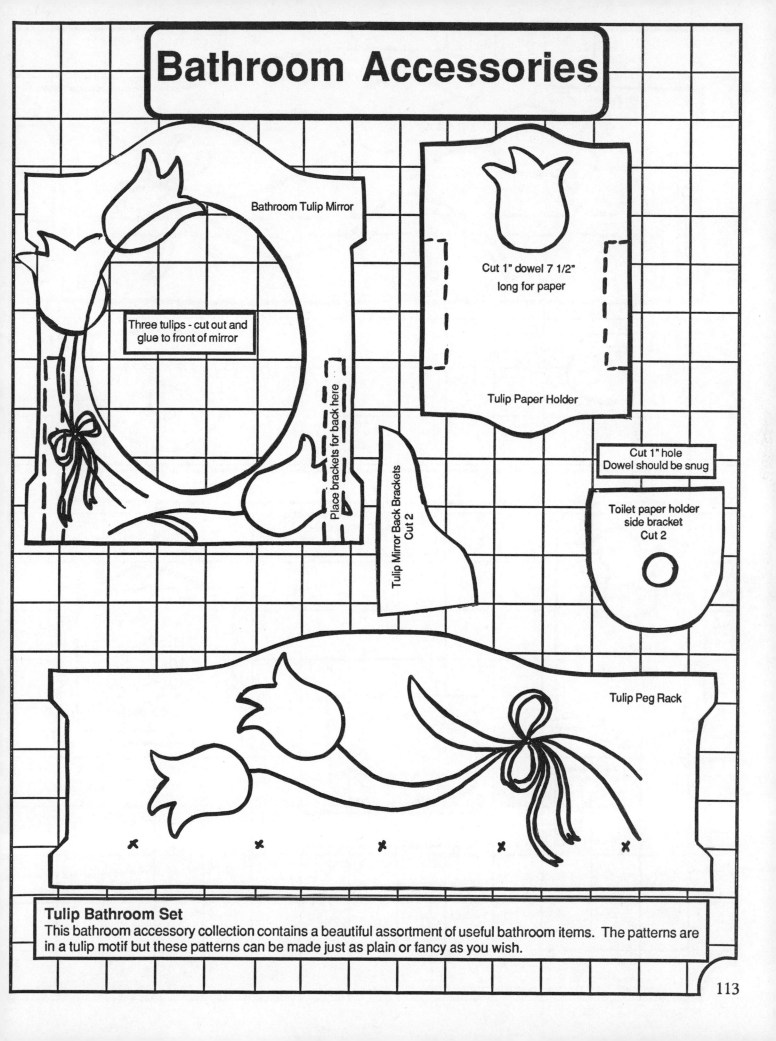

Bathroom Tulip Mirror

Three tulips - cut out and glue to front of mirror

Place brackets for back here

Cut 1" dowel 7 1/2" long for paper

Tulip Paper Holder

Tulip Mirror Back Brackets
Cut 2

Cut 1" hole
Dowel should be snug

Toilet paper holder
side bracket
Cut 2

Tulip Peg Rack

Tulip Bathroom Set
This bathroom accessory collection contains a beautiful assortment of useful bathroom items. The patterns are in a tulip motif but these patterns can be made just as plain or fancy as you wish.

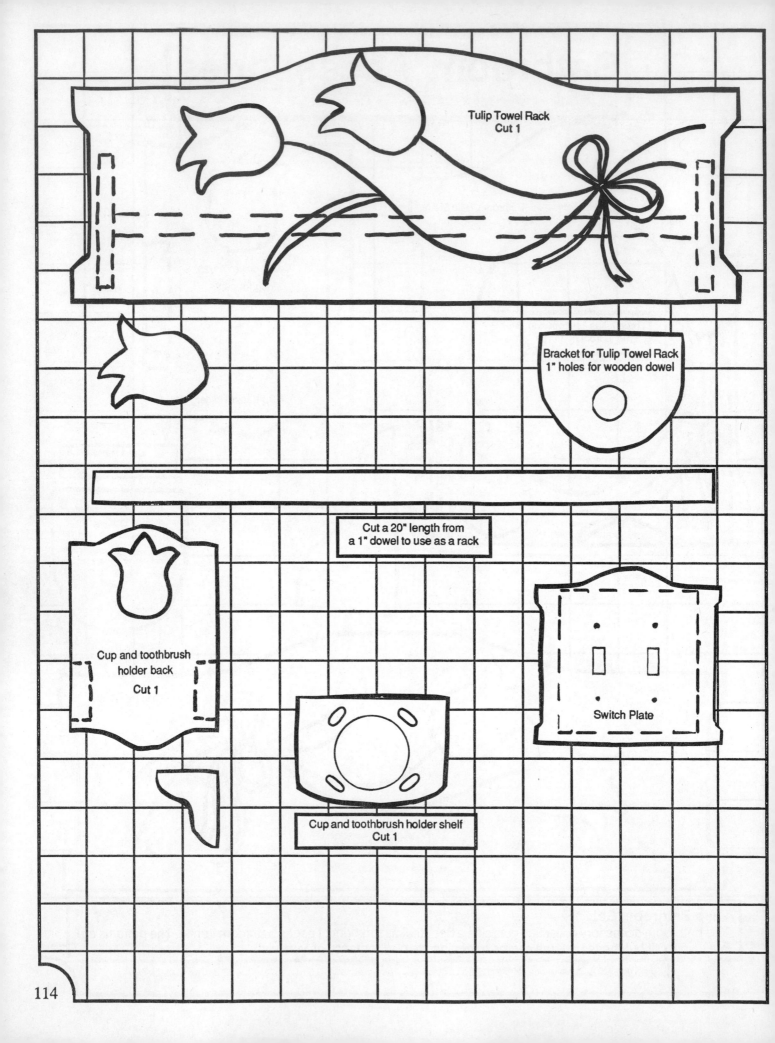

Tulip Towel Rack
Cut 1

Bracket for Tulip Towel Rack
1" holes for wooden dowel

Cut a 20" length from
a 1" dowel to use as a rack

Cup and toothbrush
holder back

Cut 1

Switch Plate

Cup and toothbrush holder shelf
Cut 1

Projects & Other Useful Accessories

Flower Basket Fireplace Insert
Cut out from 3/4" wood. Cut an 8" x 12" triangle and glue to back for support. Paint in flowers, cut out fabric or wallpaper and decoupage. Paint the basket a honey color using darker colors to shade. Simulate basketweave with fine brown lines, draw in some actual weave.

1 square = 1 - 1/2"

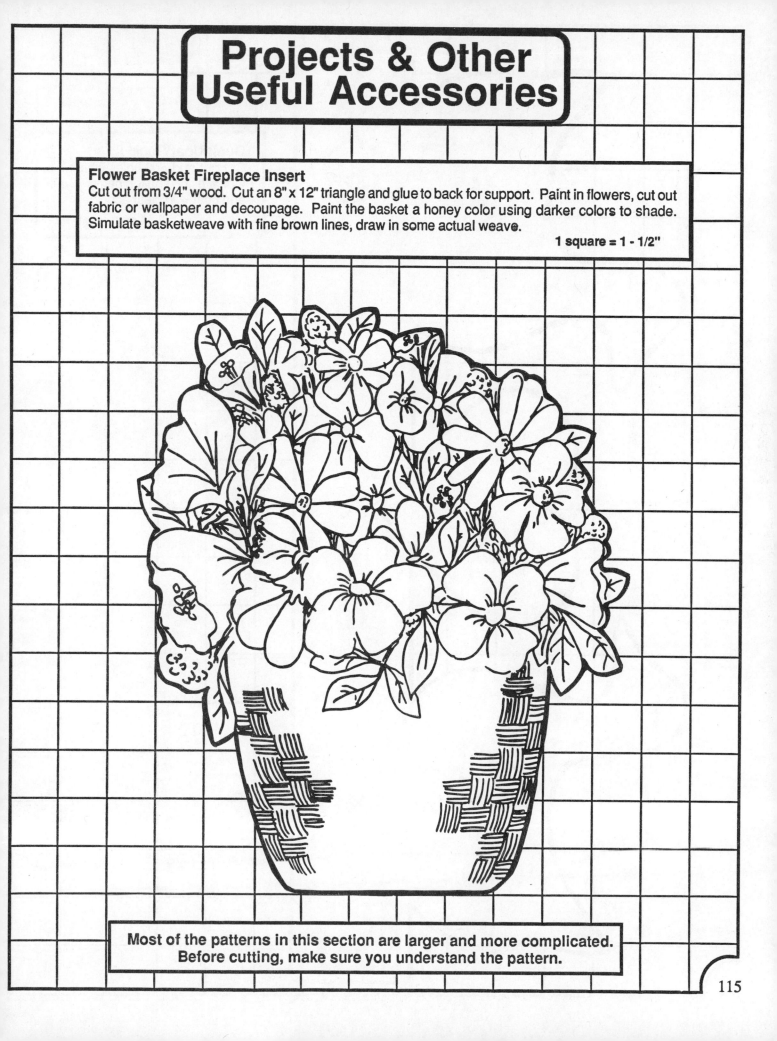

Most of the patterns in this section are larger and more complicated.
Before cutting, make sure you understand the pattern.

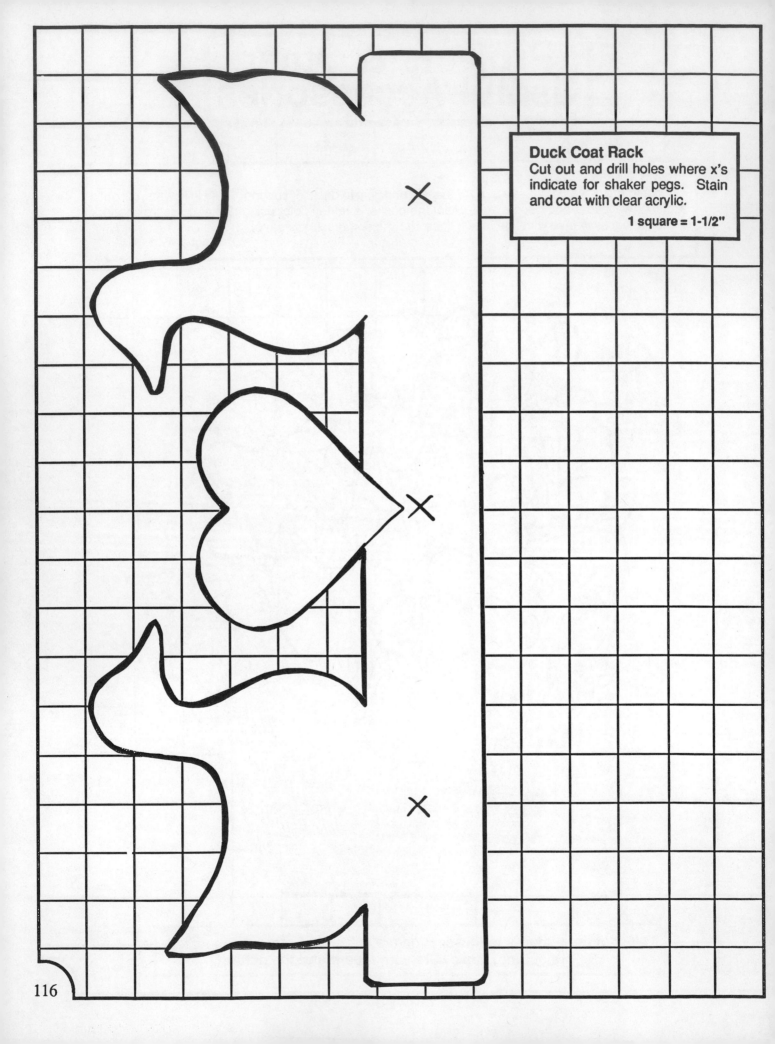

Duck Coat Rack
Cut out and drill holes where x's indicate for shaker pegs. Stain and coat with clear acrylic.

1 square = 1-1/2"

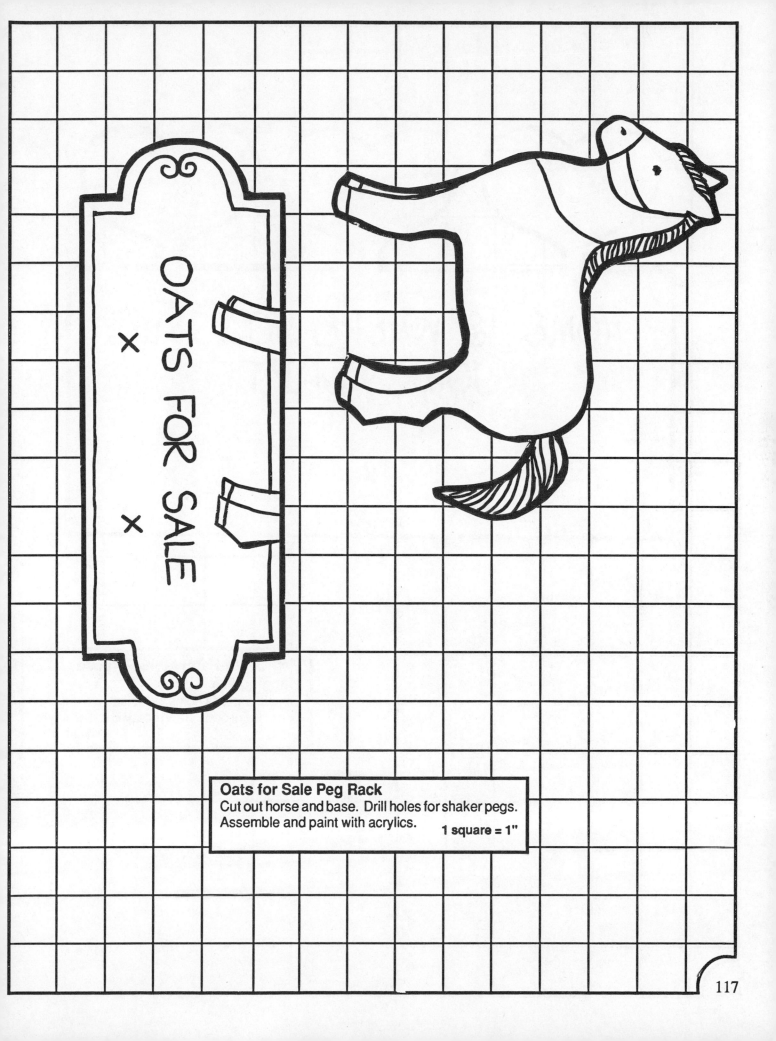

Oats for Sale Peg Rack
Cut out horse and base. Drill holes for shaker pegs.
Assemble and paint with acrylics. **1 square = 1"**

117

HOME IS WHERE YOU HANG YOUR HEART

Peg-Of-My-Heart Multi-Purpose Hanging Rack

Cut out and drill holes as indicated for shaker pegs. Paint or stain and coat with clear acrylic.

1 square = 1"

Hugging Bear Hang-Ups

Cut out bear and 2 arms. Paint all pieces (Paint arms on both sides). Tie arms "reaching out for a hug" in front. This piece is good for a child's organizer or any country decor. Attach L-hooks for hangables.

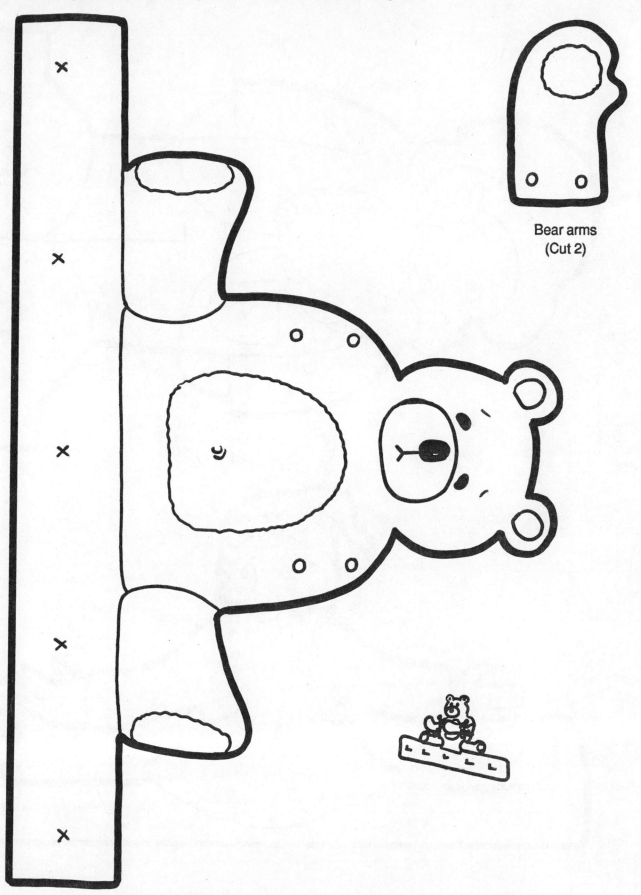

Bear arms
(Cut 2)

120

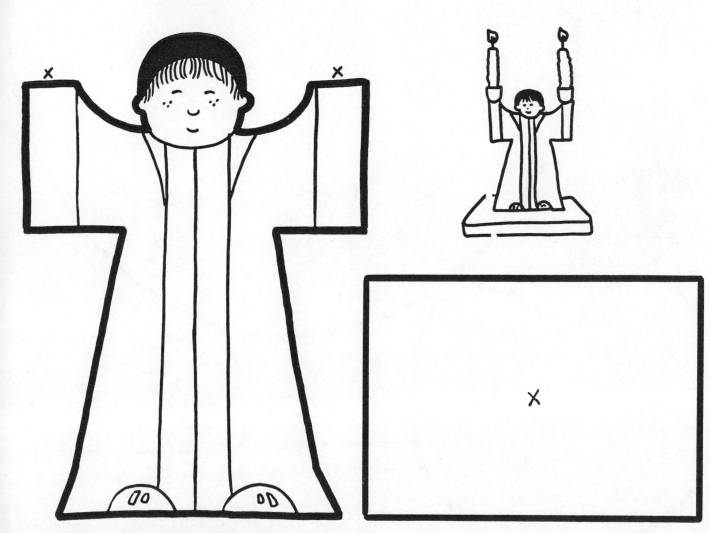

Tri-Stand Candle Holder

Cut out 3 pieces for the candle stand. Cut a small section of 1" dowel and drill a hole on one side for a candle cup holder. Assemble by gluing the three legs to the dowel and inserting the candle cup holder on top. Stain and it's ready for a candle.

Choir Boy Double Candle Holder

Cut out choir boy and base. Attach together, add candle cups at x's and paint as indicated.

121

Elegant Candelabra

Cut 1 base. Cut 3 pieces of 7/8" dowel (1-6" piece, 1-9" piece, and 1-12" piece). Attach candle cups to top of each dowel. Stain or paint. Decorate with greenery or baby's breath.

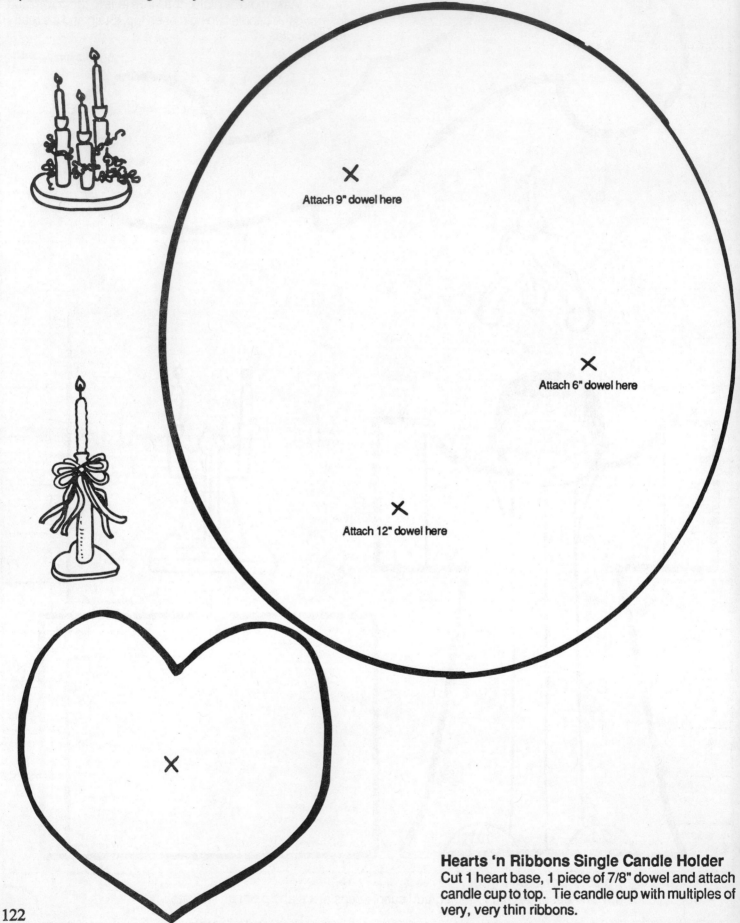

✕
Attach 9" dowel here

✕
Attach 6" dowel here

✕
Attach 12" dowel here

✕

Hearts 'n Ribbons Single Candle Holder

Cut 1 heart base, 1 piece of 7/8" dowel and attach candle cup to top. Tie candle cup with multiples of very, very thin ribbons.

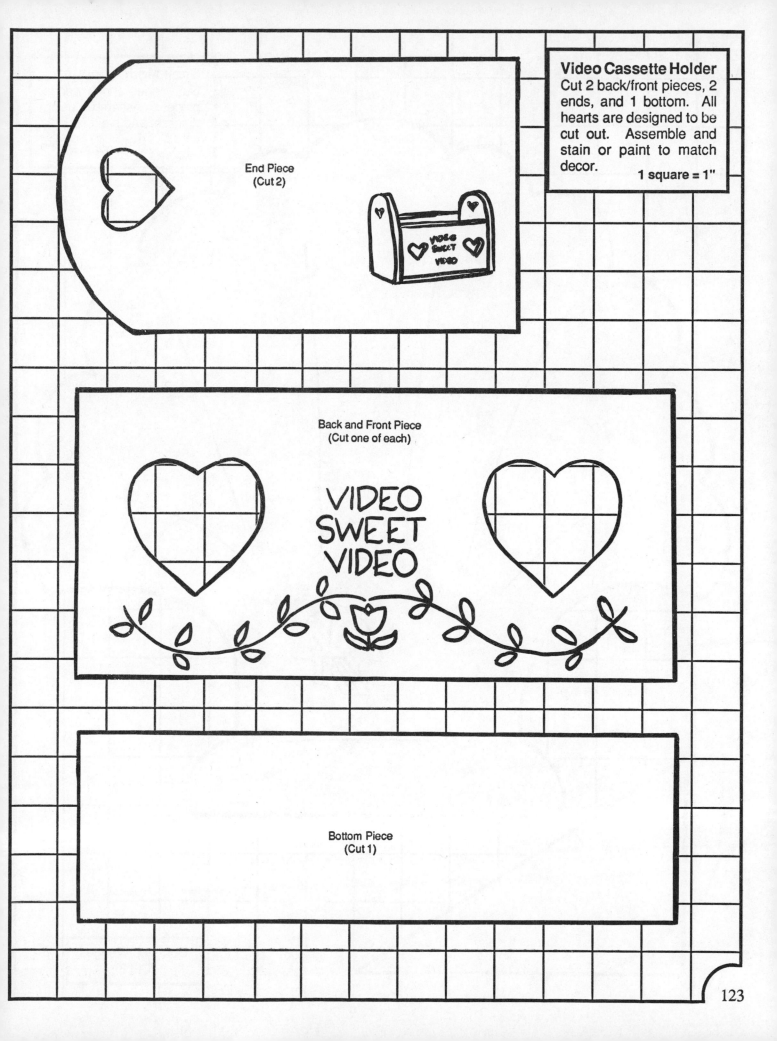

End Piece
(Cut 2)

Video Cassette Holder
Cut 2 back/front pieces, 2 ends, and 1 bottom. All hearts are designed to be cut out. Assemble and stain or paint to match decor.
1 square = 1"

Back and Front Piece
(Cut one of each)

VIDEO
SWEET
VIDEO

Bottom Piece
(Cut 1)

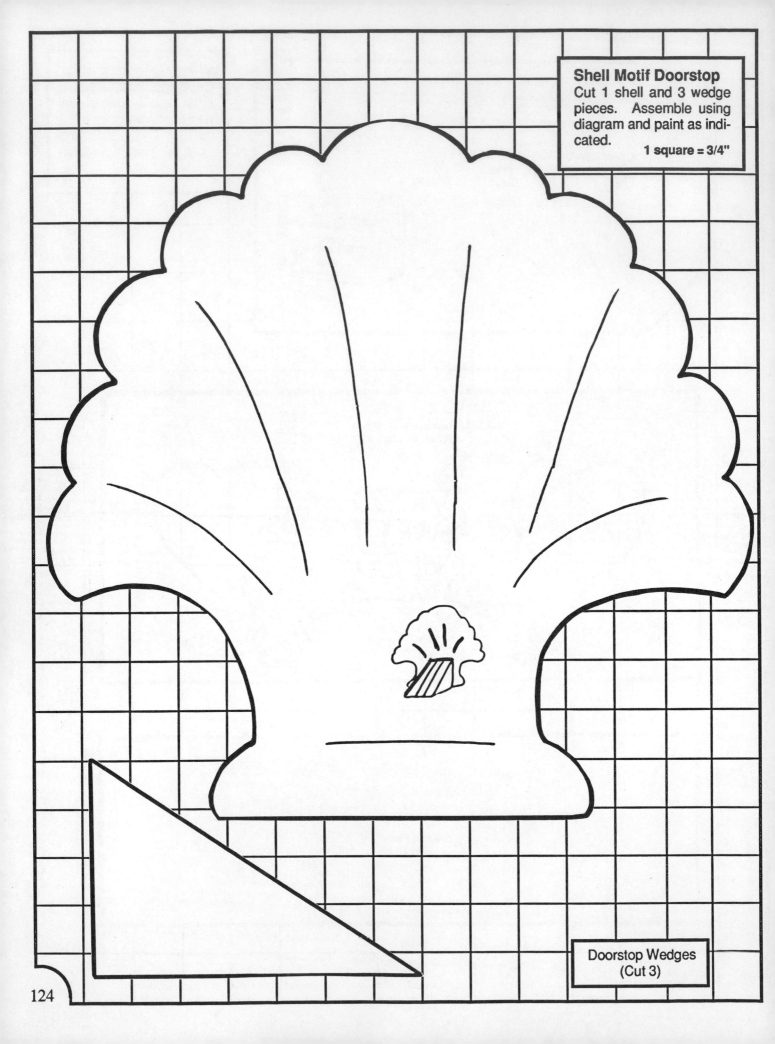

Doorstop Wedges
(Cut 3)

Amish Seamstress Door Stop
Cut 1 front and 3 braces. Assemble
and paint as indicated.
1 square = 3/4"

125

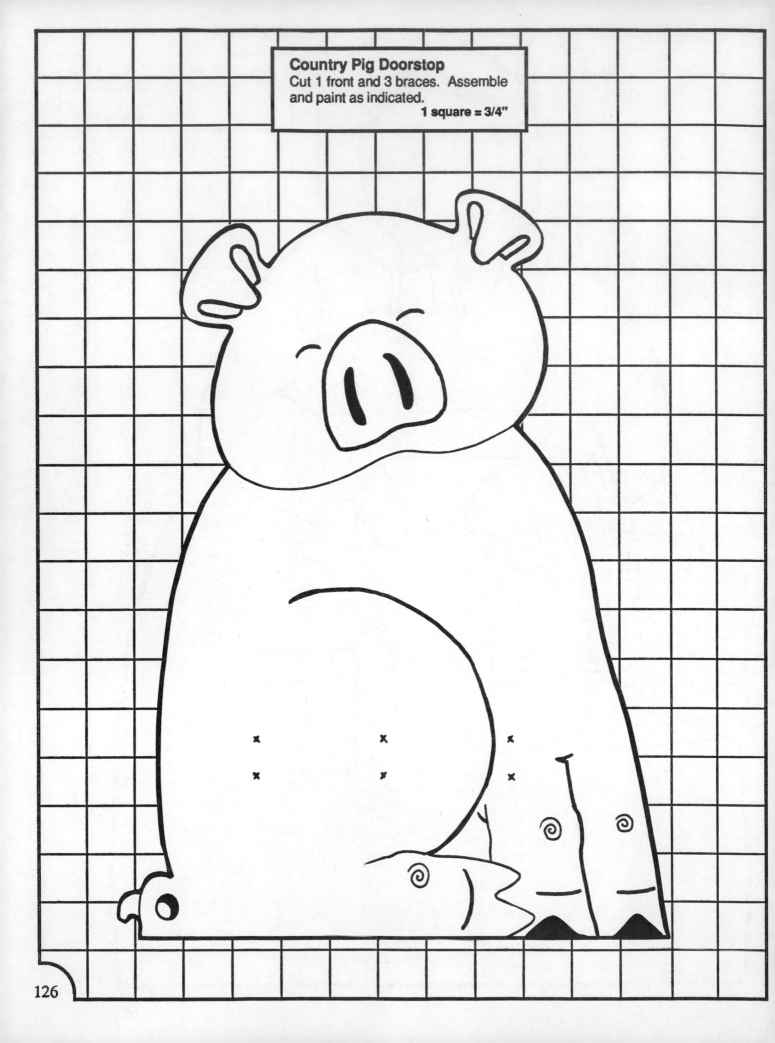

Country Pig Doorstop
Cut 1 front and 3 braces. Assemble and paint as indicated.

1 square = 3/4"

126

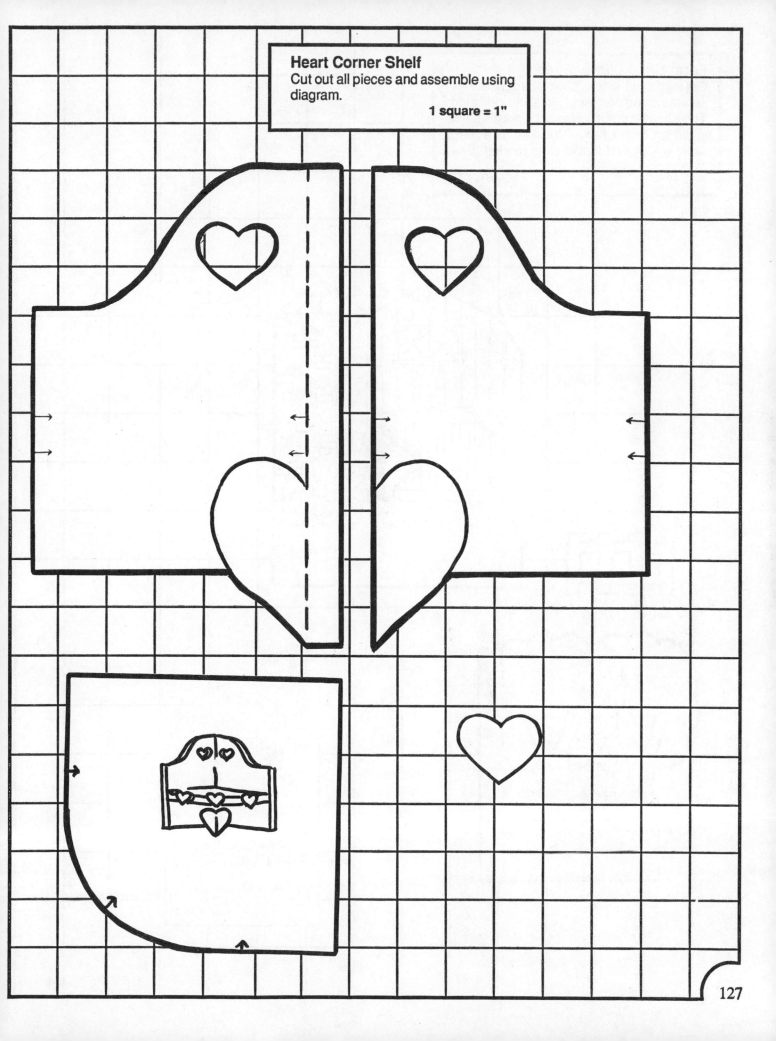

Heart Corner Shelf
Cut out all pieces and assemble using diagram.

1 square = 1"

127

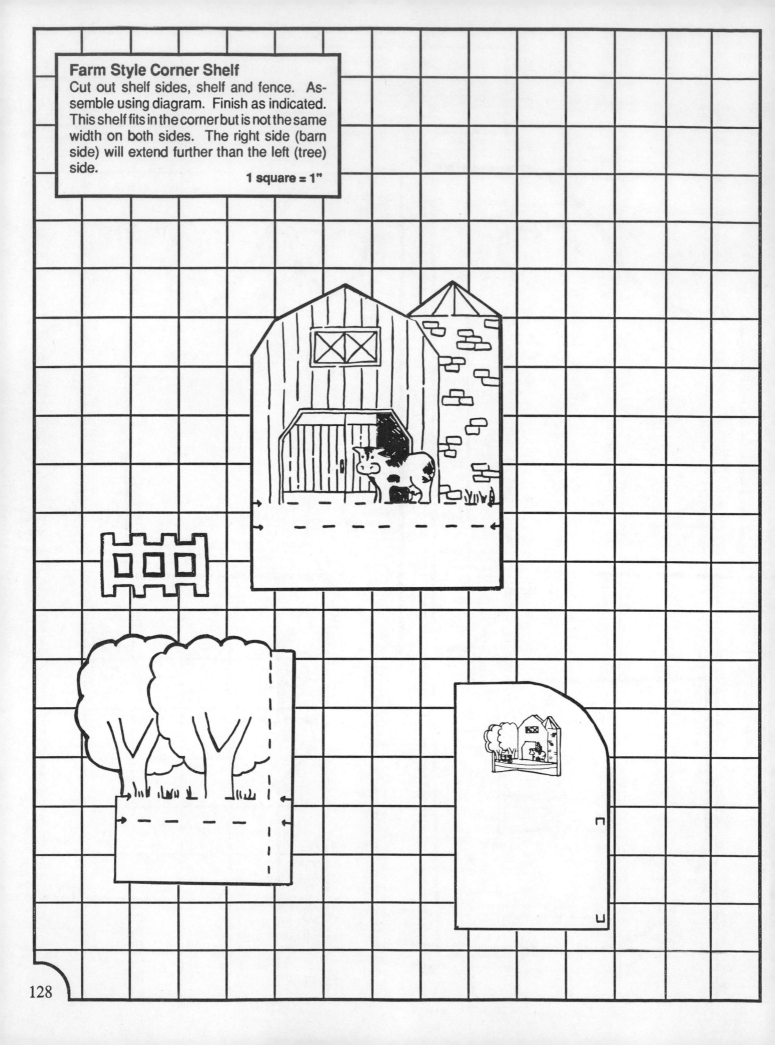

Farm Style Corner Shelf

Cut out shelf sides, shelf and fence. Assemble using diagram. Finish as indicated. This shelf fits in the corner but is not the same width on both sides. The right side (barn side) will extend further than the left (tree) side.

1 square = 1"

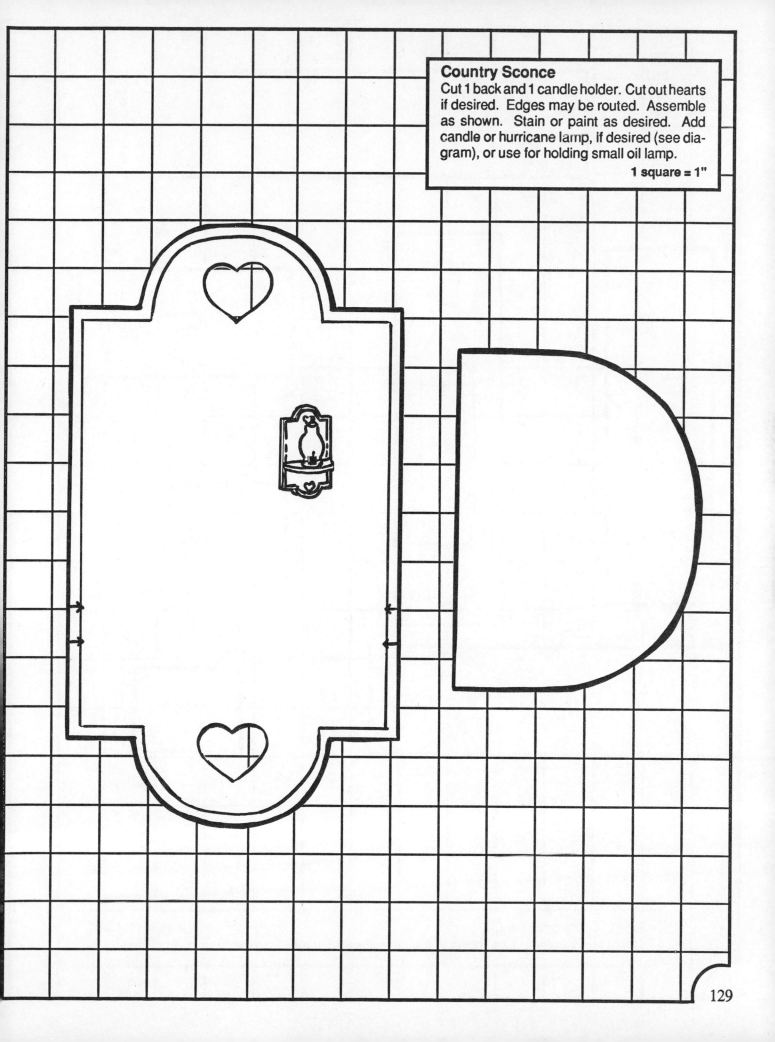

Country Sconce

Cut 1 back and 1 candle holder. Cut out hearts if desired. Edges may be routed. Assemble as shown. Stain or paint as desired. Add candle or hurricane lamp, if desired (see diagram), or use for holding small oil lamp.

1 square = 1"

129

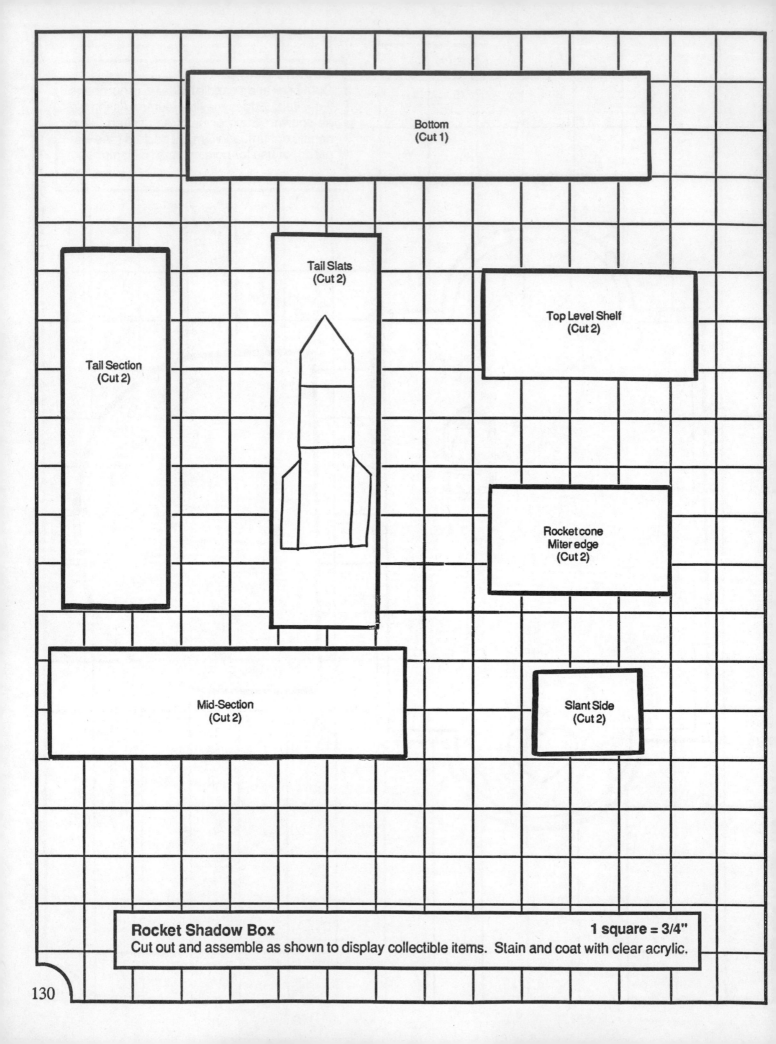

Bottom
(Cut 1)

Tail Slats
(Cut 2)

Top Level Shelf
(Cut 2)

Tail Section
(Cut 2)

Rocket cone
Miter edge
(Cut 2)

Mid-Section
(Cut 2)

Slant Side
(Cut 2)

Rocket Shadow Box
Cut out and assemble as shown to display collectible items. Stain and coat with clear acrylic.

1 square = 3/4"

130

Southwestern Design Shelf/Sconce

This pattern could be used as a small shelf to hold figures or plants, or as a sconce or votive candle holder. Cut out and assemble as shown. Paint in desert colors.

1 square = 1"

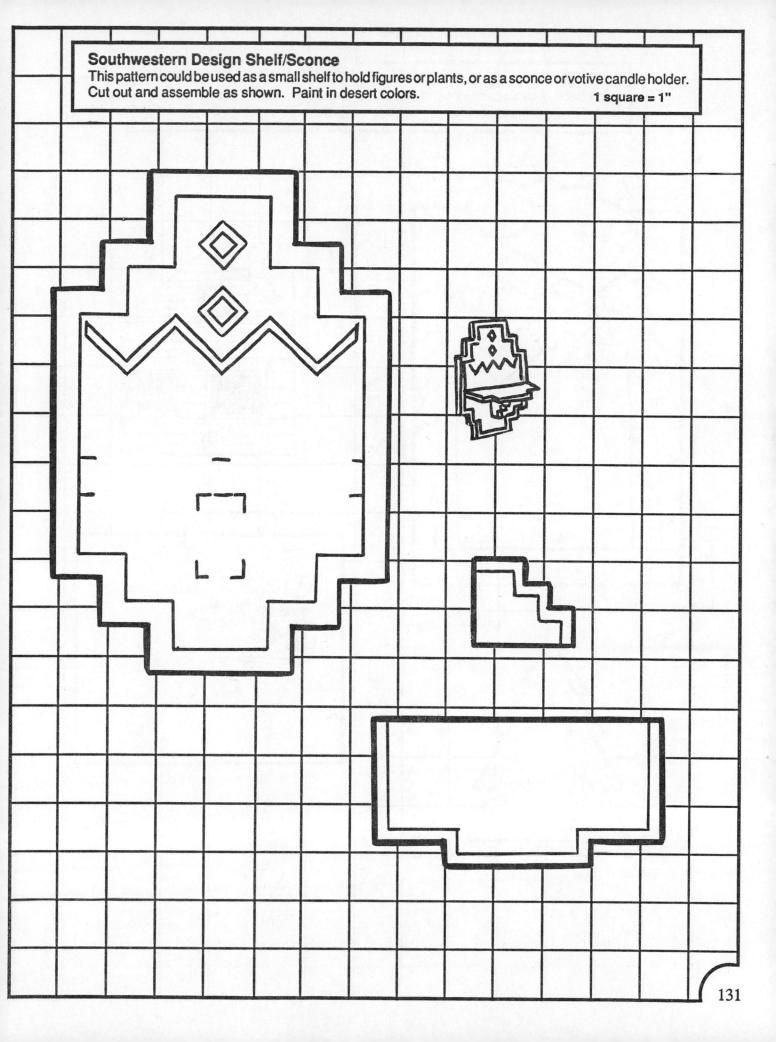

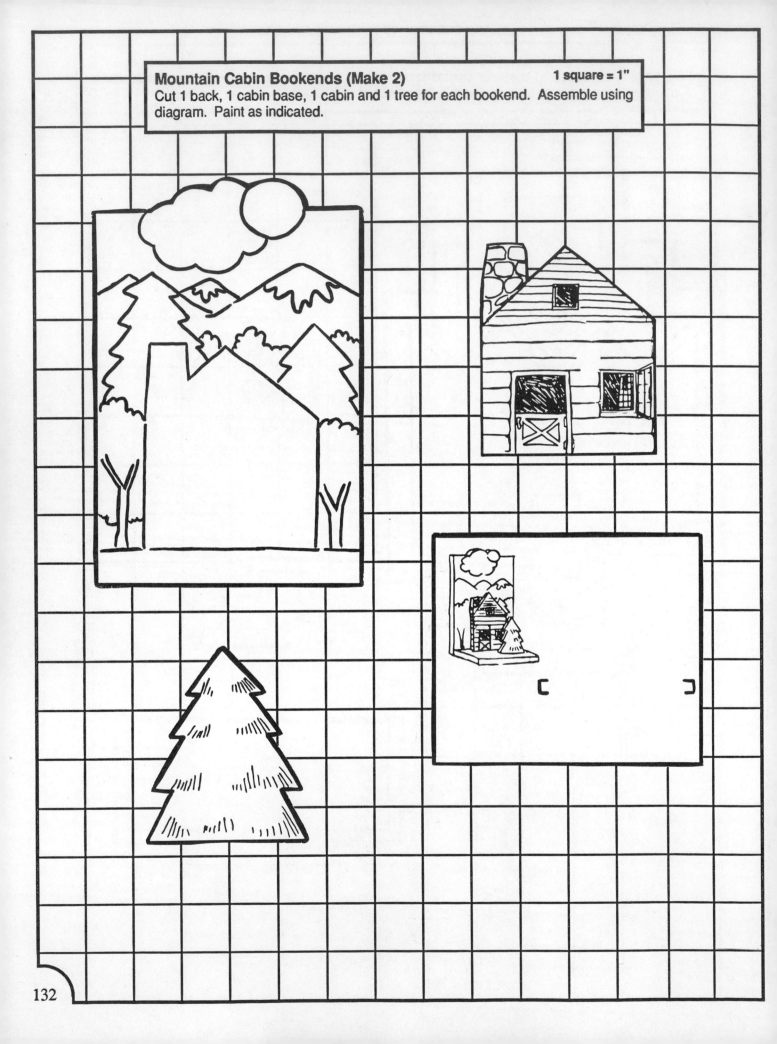

Mountain Cabin Bookends (Make 2)

1 square = 1"

Cut 1 back, 1 cabin base, 1 cabin and 1 tree for each bookend. Assemble using diagram. Paint as indicated.

132

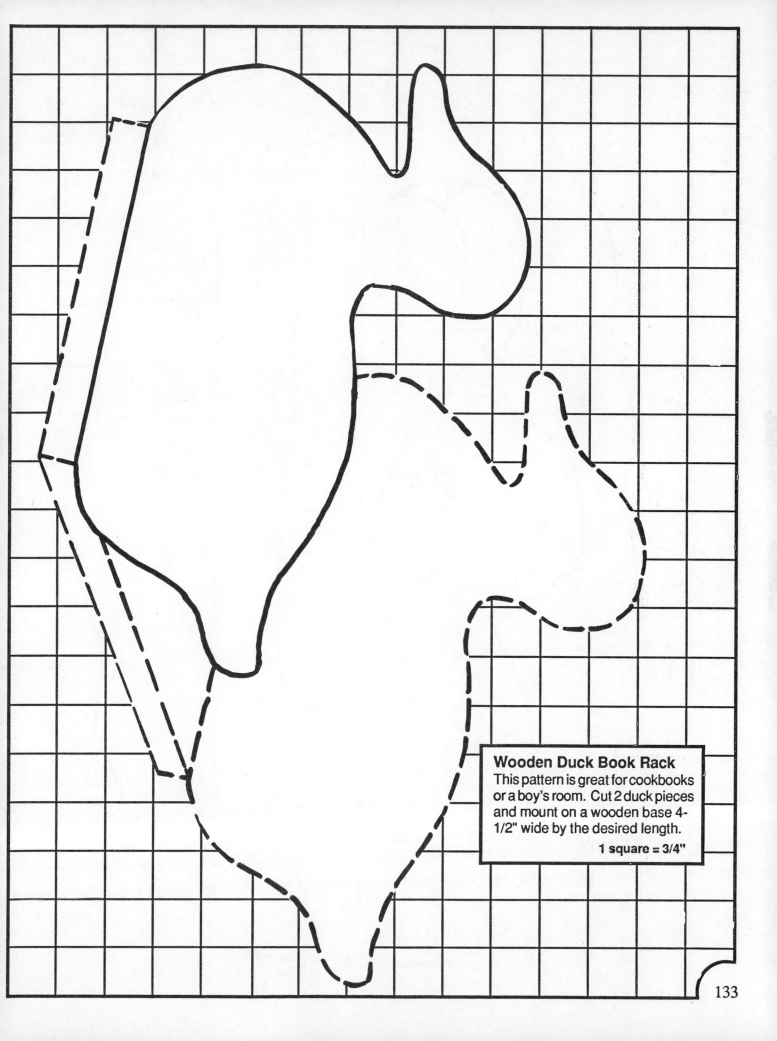

Wooden Duck Book Rack
This pattern is great for cookbooks or a boy's room. Cut 2 duck pieces and mount on a wooden base 4-1/2" wide by the desired length.

1 square = 3/4"

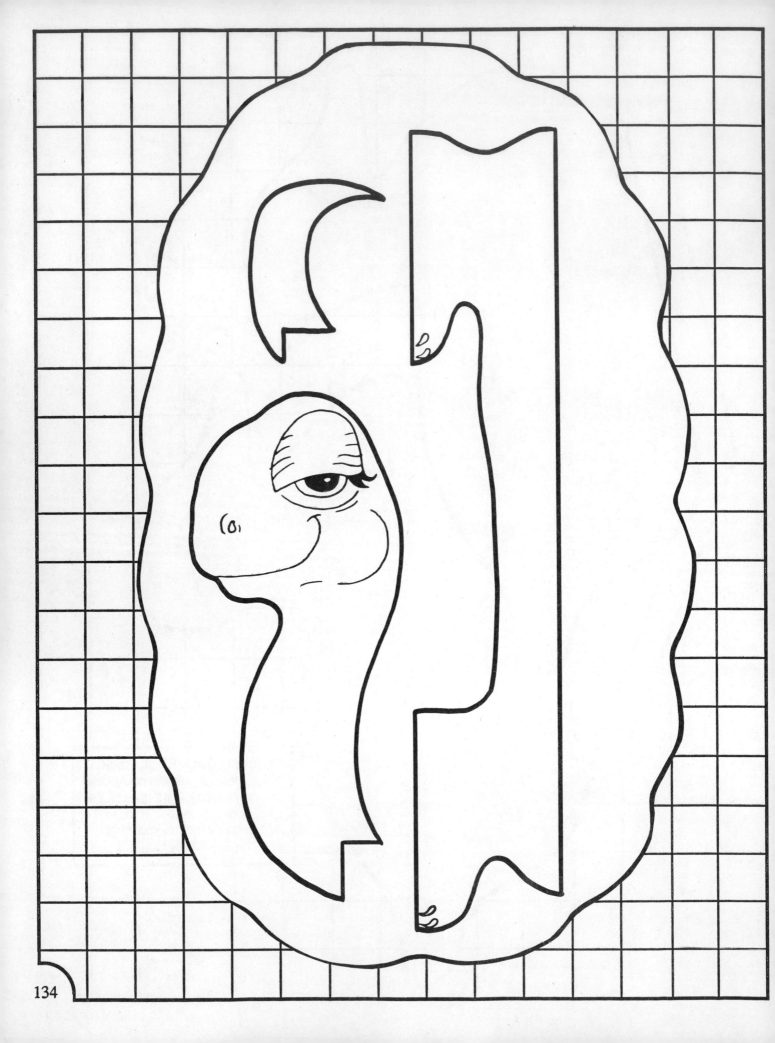

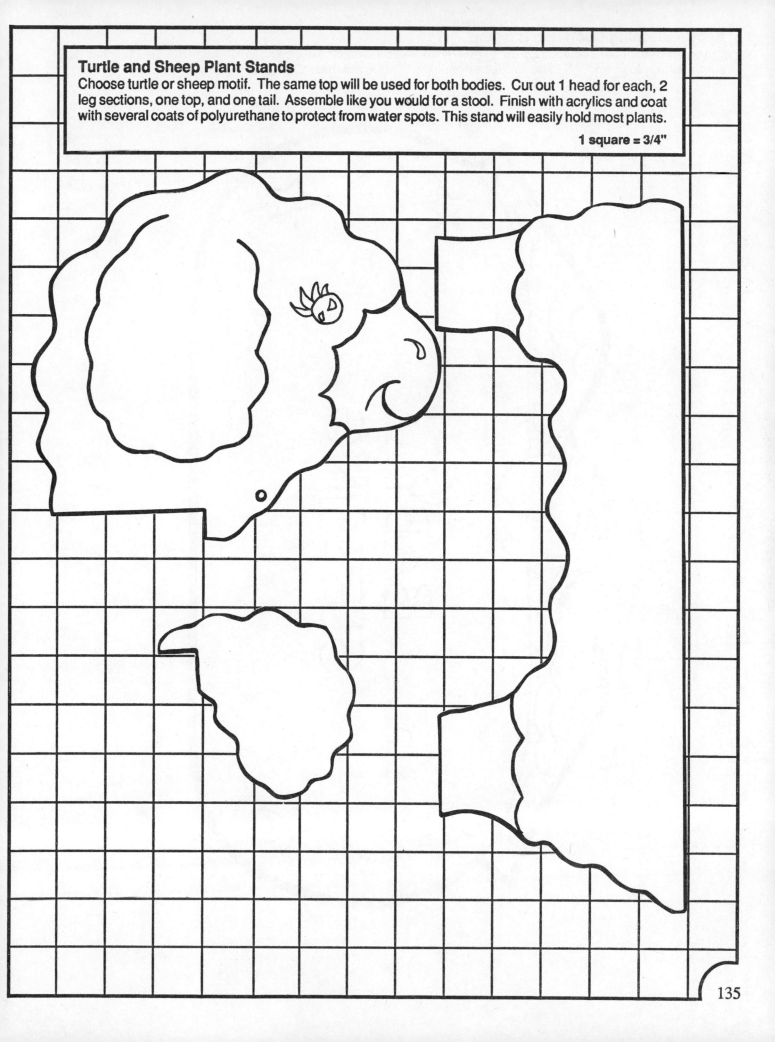

Turtle and Sheep Plant Stands
Choose turtle or sheep motif. The same top will be used for both bodies. Cut out 1 head for each, 2 leg sections, one top, and one tail. Assemble like you would for a stool. Finish with acrylics and coat with several coats of polyurethane to protect from water spots. This stand will easily hold most plants.

1 square = 3/4"

135

Baby's Sleeping Doorknob Hanging

Cut out and finish as indicated. Screw a small eye hook as indicated. Insert a ribbon through the eye hook and tie. Make sure ribbon is long enough to hang over a doorknob. This is a perfect "Do Not Disturb" sign for baby.

Switchplates
Cut from thin wood. (Don't forget to cut out for switch.) Drill holes as indicated for screws.

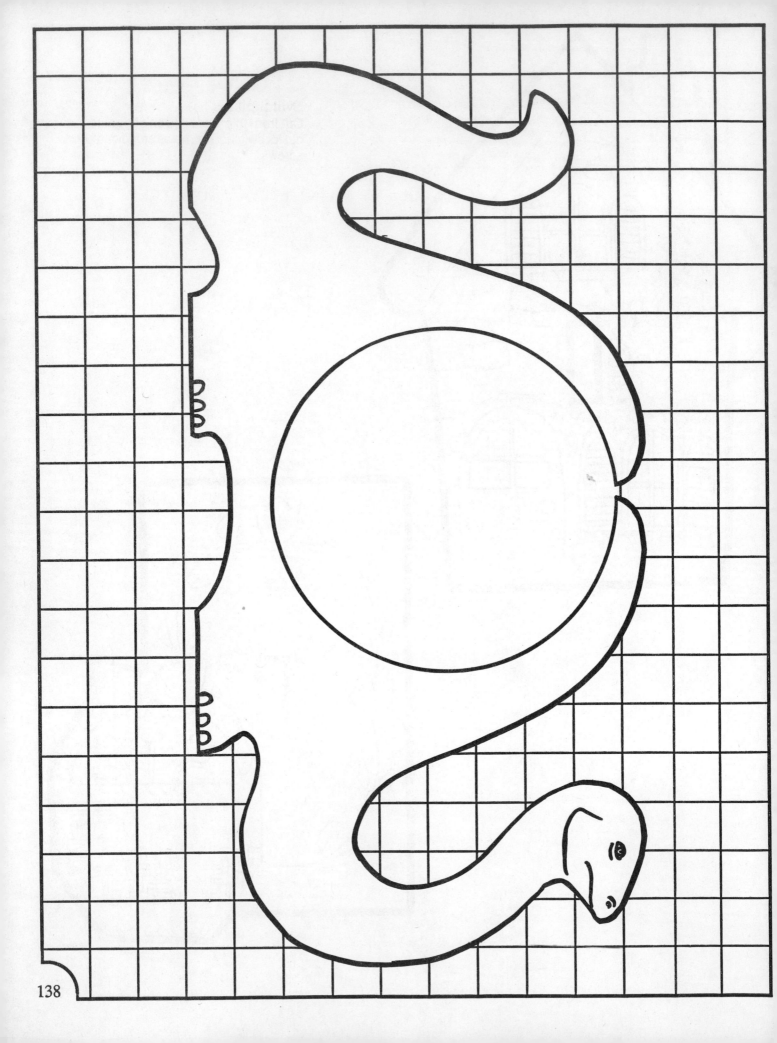

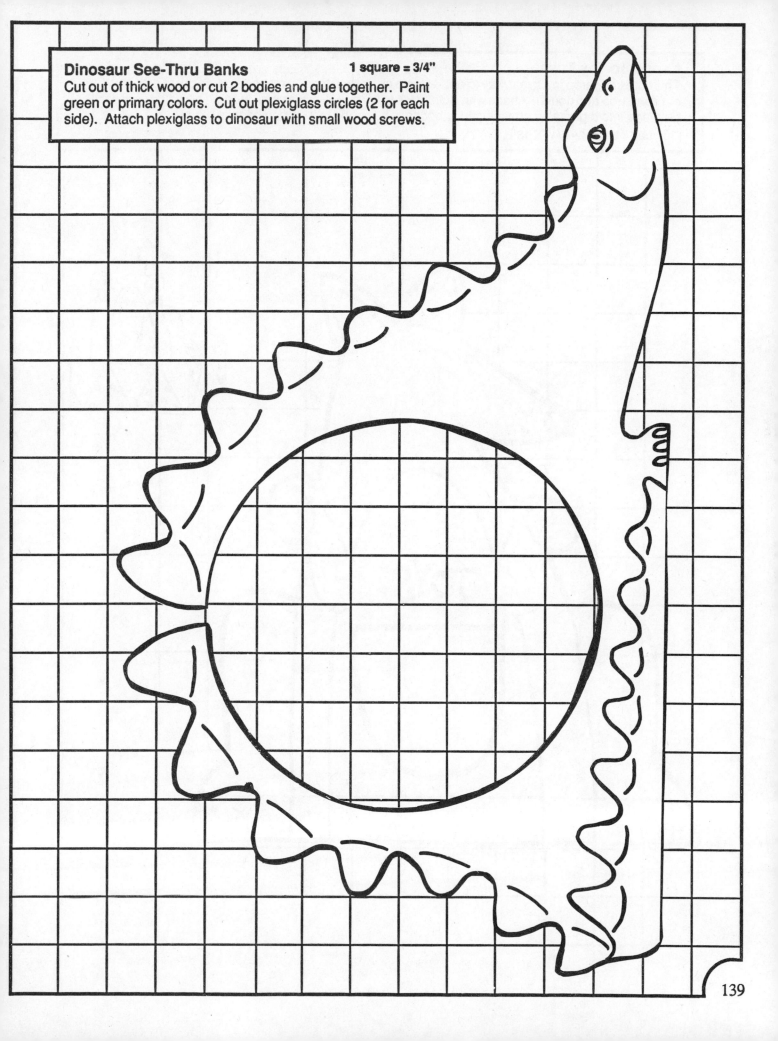

Dinosaur See-Thru Banks

1 square = 3/4"

Cut out of thick wood or cut 2 bodies and glue together. Paint green or primary colors. Cut out plexiglass circles (2 for each side). Attach plexiglass to dinosaur with small wood screws.

139

Kangaroo Toy Toss

1 square = 1 - 1/2"

This cute kangaroo is a great way to get kids to pick up their toys. It makes a game out of a chore! Cut out kangaroo and pouch. Attach with Bolts at x's to toy box. Paint as indicated. (This could very easily be made into a game by attaching to supports in back and using bean bags to toss.)

Finished Size: 15 - 3/4" X 18"

TOYS

TOYS

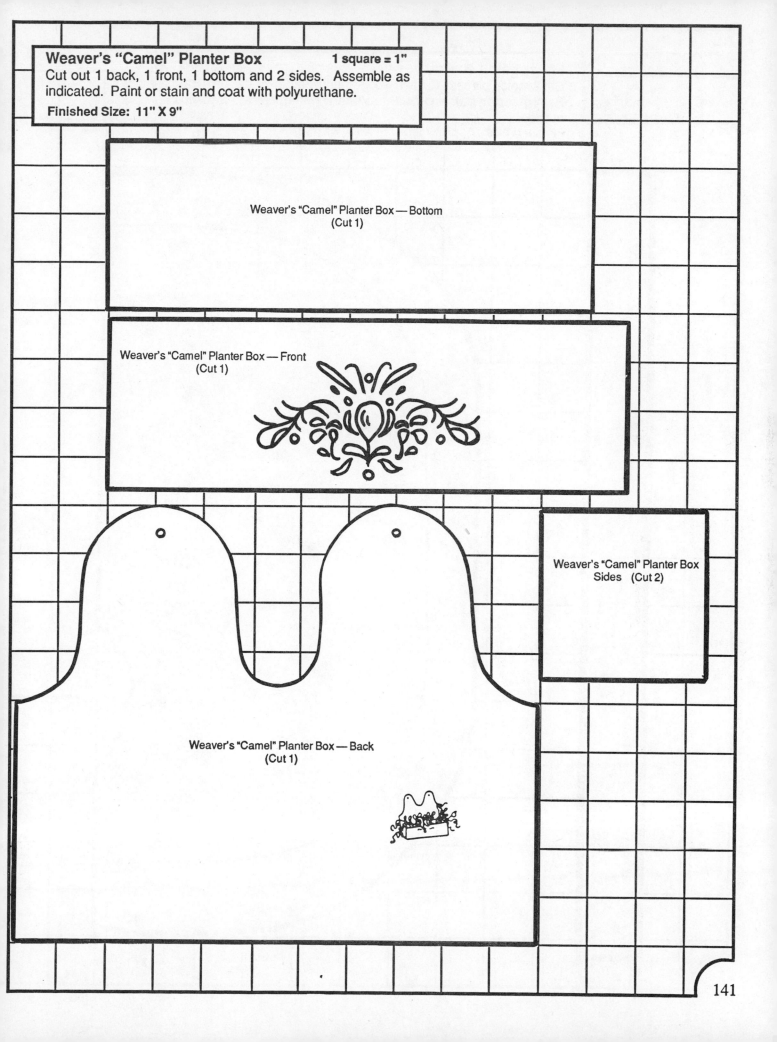

Weaver's "Camel" Planter Box

1 square = 1"

Cut out 1 back, 1 front, 1 bottom and 2 sides. Assemble as indicated. Paint or stain and coat with polyurethane.

Finished Size: 11" X 9"

Weaver's "Camel" Planter Box — Bottom
(Cut 1)

Weaver's "Camel" Planter Box — Front
(Cut 1)

Weaver's "Camel" Planter Box
Sides   (Cut 2)

Weaver's "Camel" Planter Box — Back
(Cut 1)

141

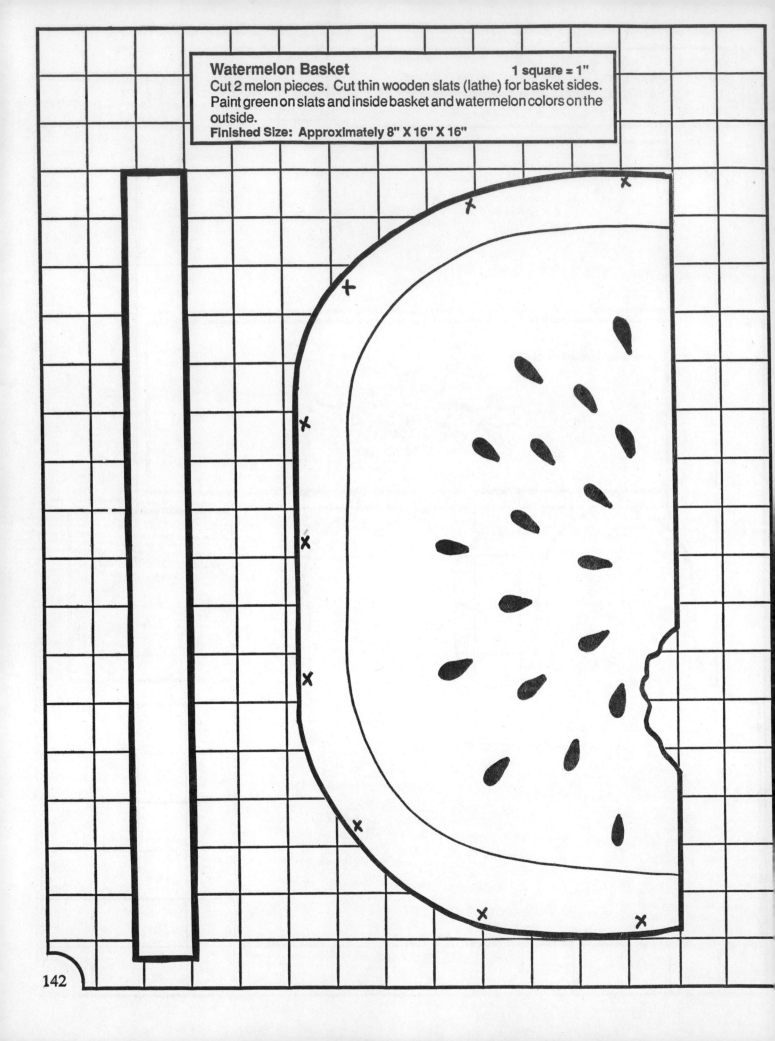

Watermelon Basket

1 square = 1"

Cut 2 melon pieces. Cut thin wooden slats (lathe) for basket sides.
Paint green on slats and inside basket and watermelon colors on the
outside.

Finished Size: Approximately 8" X 16" X 16"

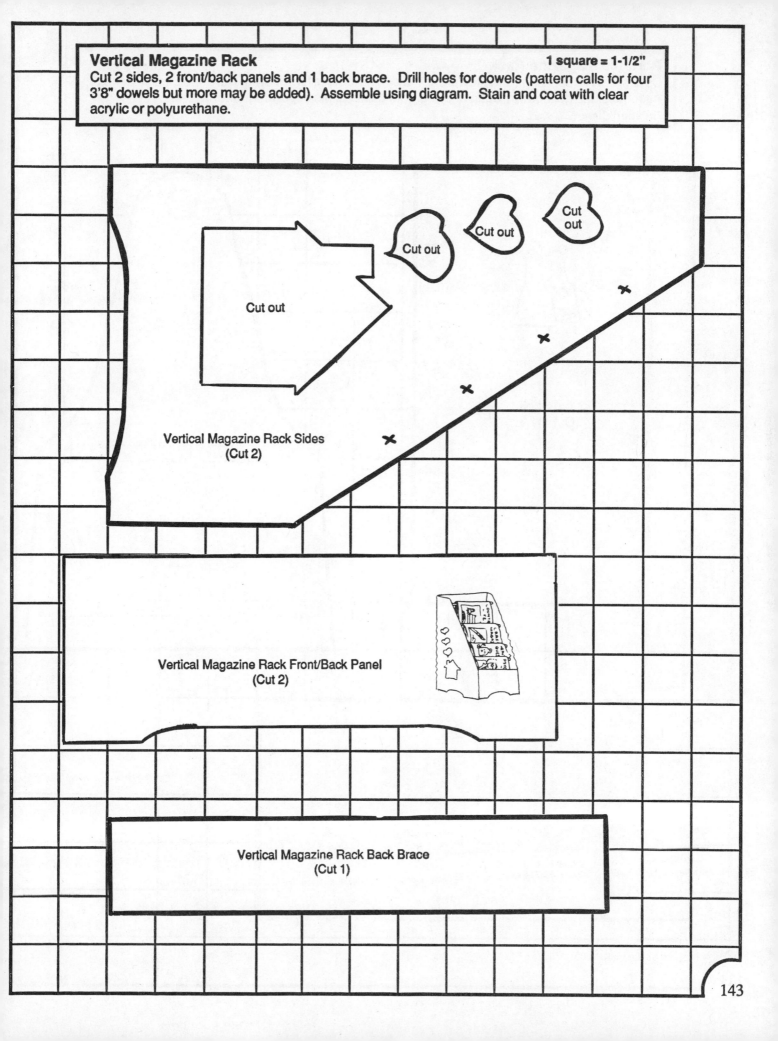

Vertical Magazine Rack

1 square = 1-1/2"

Cut 2 sides, 2 front/back panels and 1 back brace. Drill holes for dowels (pattern calls for four 3'8" dowels but more may be added). Assemble using diagram. Stain and coat with clear acrylic or polyurethane.

Cut out

Cut out

Cut out

Cut out

Vertical Magazine Rack Sides
(Cut 2)

Vertical Magazine Rack Front/Back Panel
(Cut 2)

Vertical Magazine Rack Back Brace
(Cut 1)

143

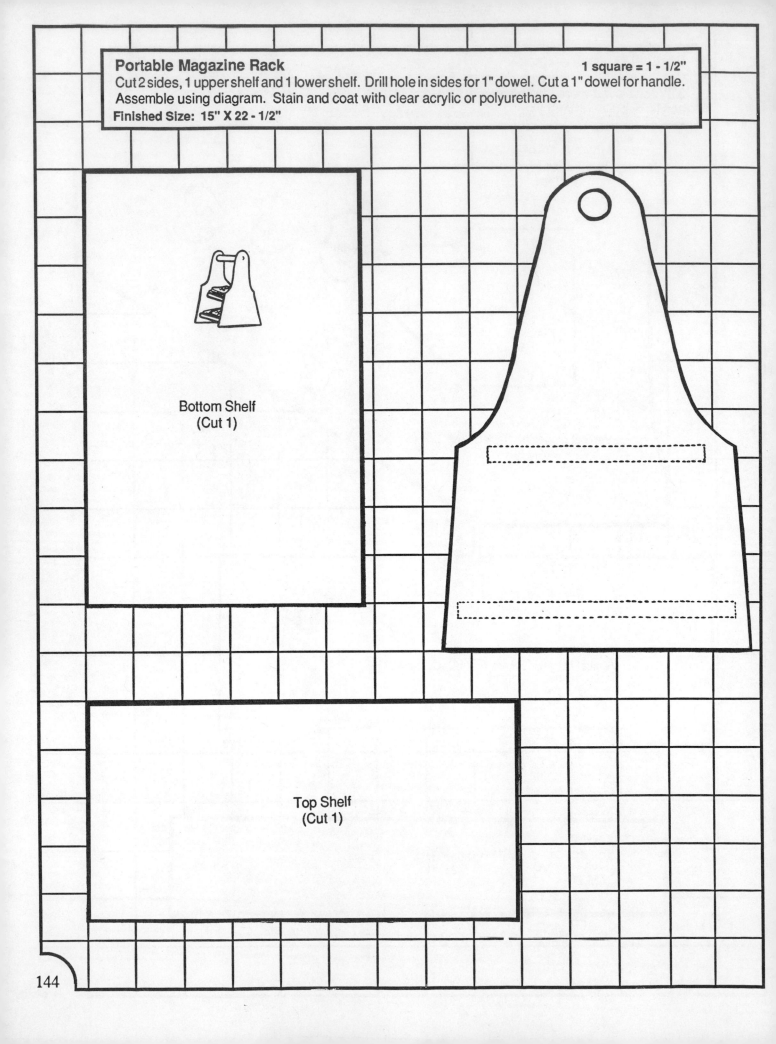

Portable Magazine Rack

1 square = 1 - 1/2"

Cut 2 sides, 1 upper shelf and 1 lower shelf. Drill hole in sides for 1" dowel. Cut a 1" dowel for handle. Assemble using diagram. Stain and coat with clear acrylic or polyurethane.

Finished Size: 15" X 22 - 1/2"

Bottom Shelf
(Cut 1)

Top Shelf
(Cut 1)

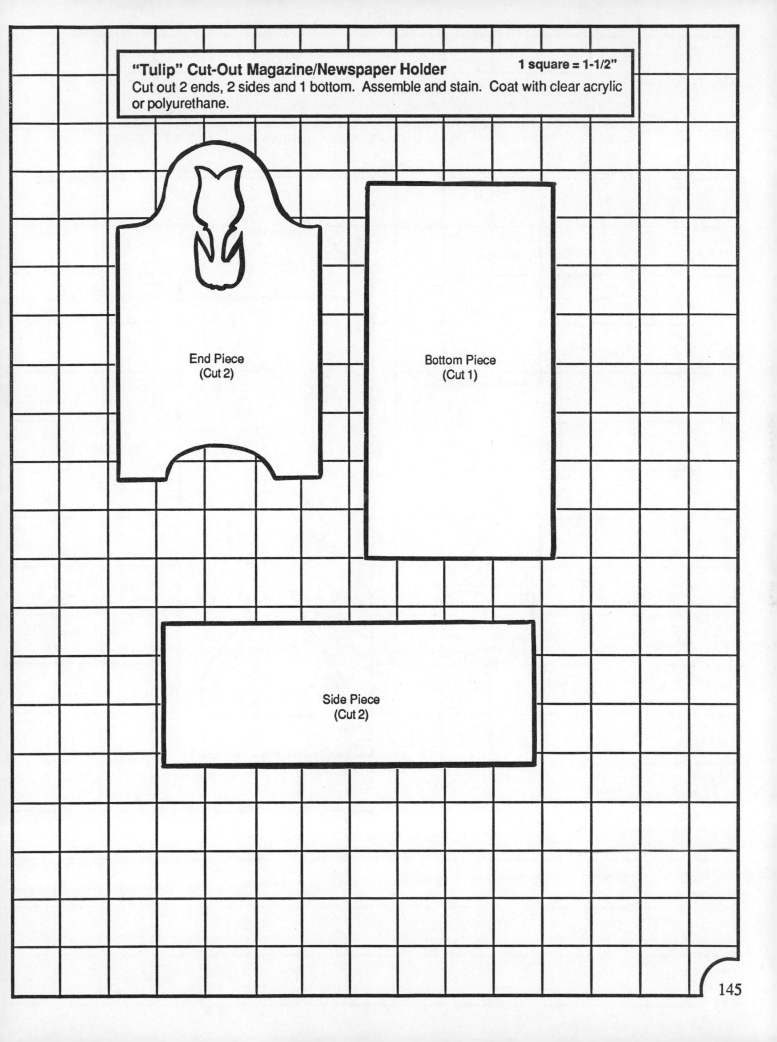

"Tulip" Cut-Out Magazine/Newspaper Holder

1 square = 1-1/2"

Cut out 2 ends, 2 sides and 1 bottom. Assemble and stain. Coat with clear acrylic or polyurethane.

End Piece
(Cut 2)

Bottom Piece
(Cut 1)

Side Piece
(Cut 2)

Combination Letter/Key/Message Holder

1 square = 1"

Cut out 1 back, 1 letter holder front and 1 letter holder bottom. Assemble using diagram. Letter holder bottom attaches to the back and the front extends outward from the bottom. Stain or paint. Attach a square of cork with glue and this multi-purpose accessory will be complete.

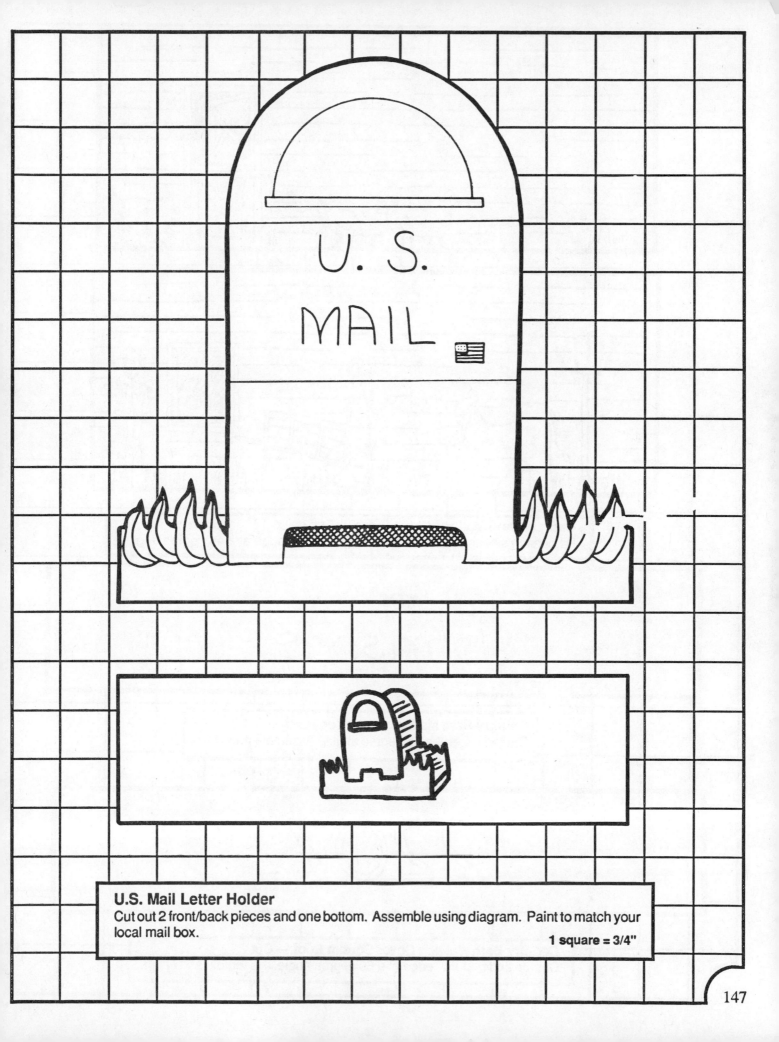

U.S. Mail Letter Holder
Cut out 2 front/back pieces and one bottom. Assemble using diagram. Paint to match your local mail box.

1 square = 3/4"

Country Barn Mailbox Cover Sides — Cut 2
Paint each side the same as shown. Cut the top edge at a 45 degree angle.

the

Johnsons

Country Barn Mailbox Cover Top Roof — Cut 2
Cut top edge at a 45 degree angle. Assemble and finish.

2207

Country Barn Mailbox Cover Bottom Roof — Cut 2
Cut top and bottom   edge at a 60 degree angle. Assemble and finish.

Country Barn Mailbox Cover

1 square = 1-1/2"

This mailbox cover makes a nice welcomer. Cut 2 sides, 2 top roof pieces, 2 bottom roof pieces, 1 back, 1 flag and 1 bottom. Assemble all pieces, except bottom. After assembly is complete measure for the bottom (the size will depend on the thickness of the wood you use. Cut roof pieces at an angle to fit properly. Use a regular size mailbox. Paint barn front on the metal mailbox door. Finish by painting as shown. Paint red or country blue. Use several coats of exterior polyurethane as a finish to protect from weathering. Coat annually with polyurethane. Attach flag. Place on a standard mailbox post and slide in mailbox.

Mailbox Flag
Paint red or as American Flag. Drill hole and slot at base and attach with screw to mailbox side. Flag will turn on screw and the slot will keep it stationary for mail pick up.

Country Barn Mailbox Cover Back — Cut 1

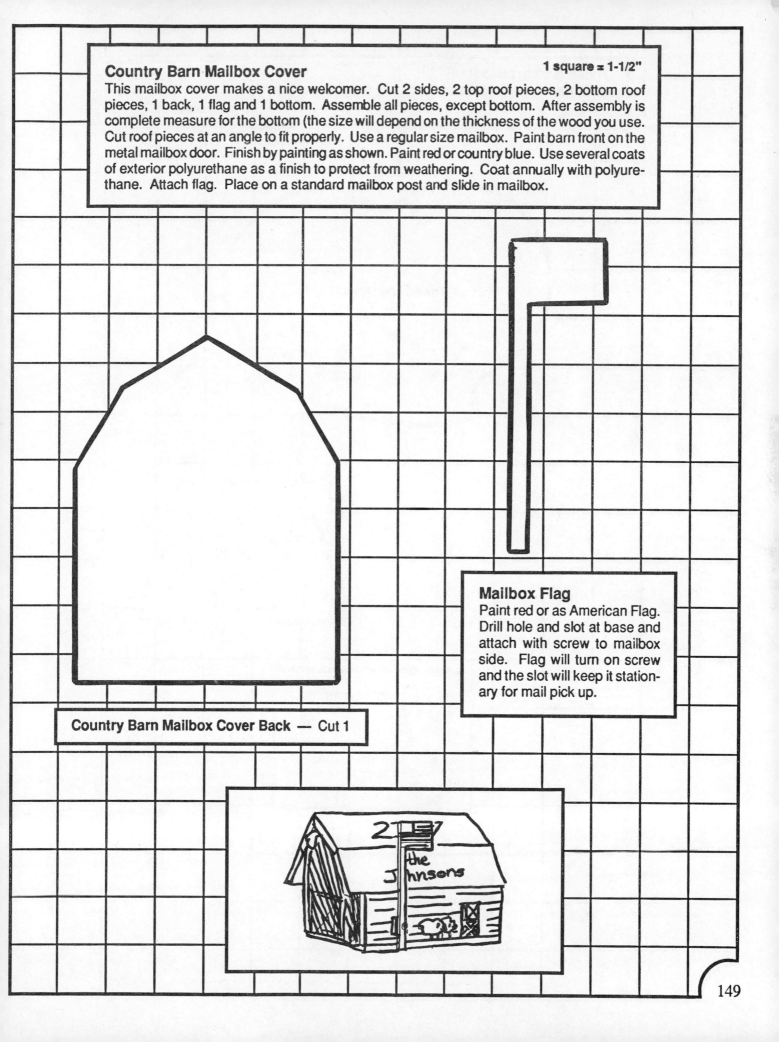

149

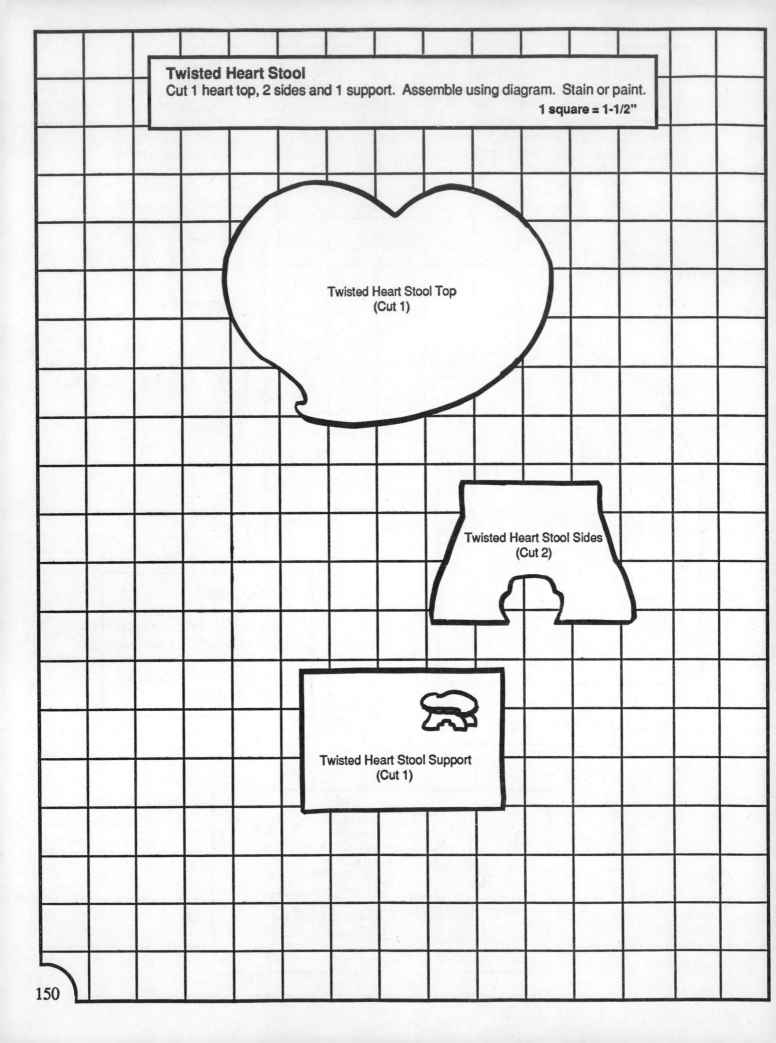

Twisted Heart Stool
Cut 1 heart top, 2 sides and 1 support. Assemble using diagram. Stain or paint.

1 square = 1-1/2"

Twisted Heart Stool Top
(Cut 1)

Twisted Heart Stool Sides
(Cut 2)

Twisted Heart Stool Support
(Cut 1)

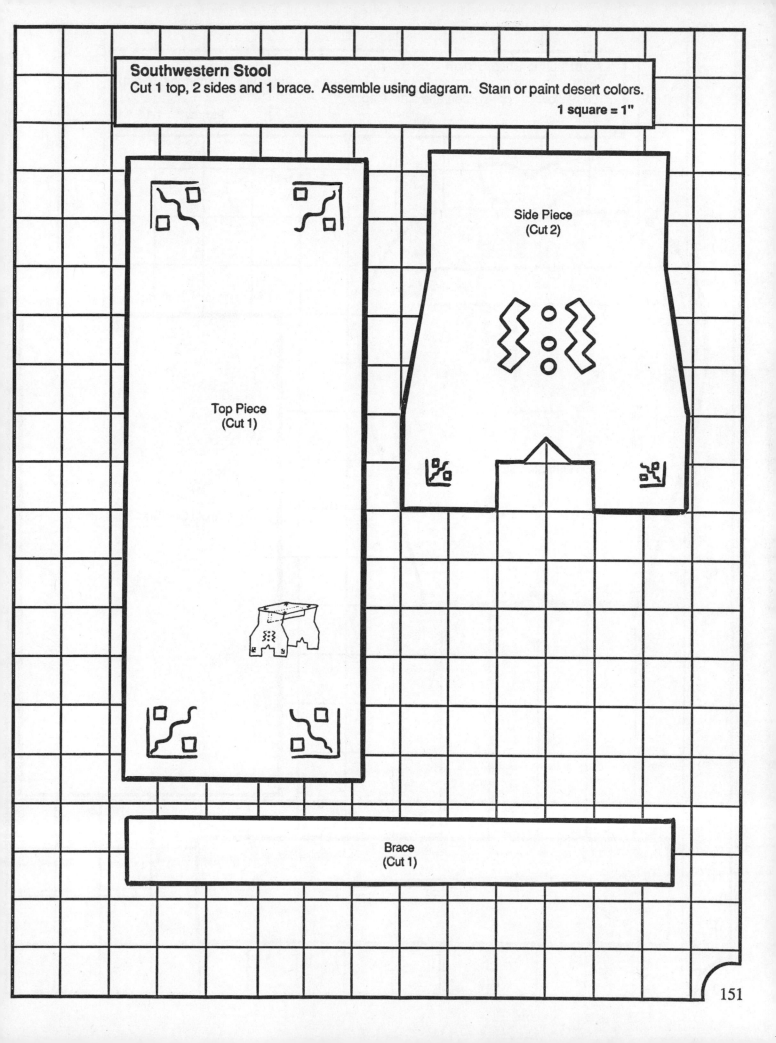

Southwestern Stool
Cut 1 top, 2 sides and 1 brace. Assemble using diagram. Stain or paint desert colors.

1 square = 1"

Top Piece
(Cut 1)

Side Piece
(Cut 2)

Brace
(Cut 1)

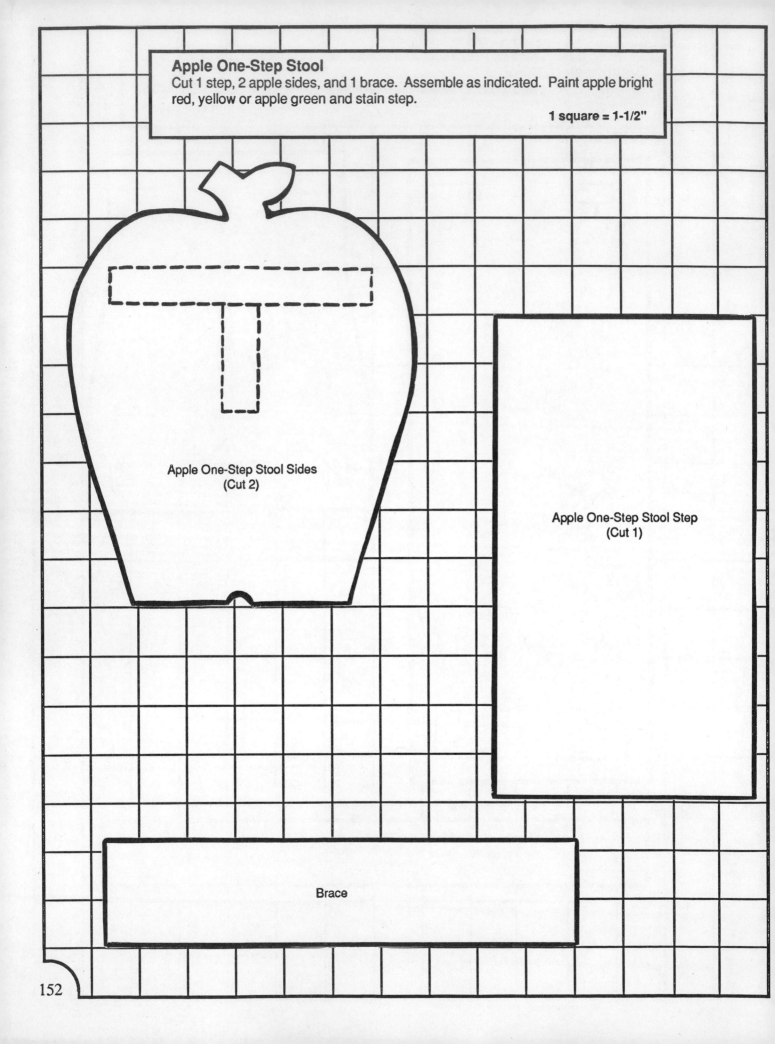

Apple One-Step Stool

Cut 1 step, 2 apple sides, and 1 brace. Assemble as indicated. Paint apple bright red, yellow or apple green and stain step.

1 square = 1-1/2"

Apple One-Step Stool Sides
(Cut 2)

Apple One-Step Stool Step
(Cut 1)

Brace

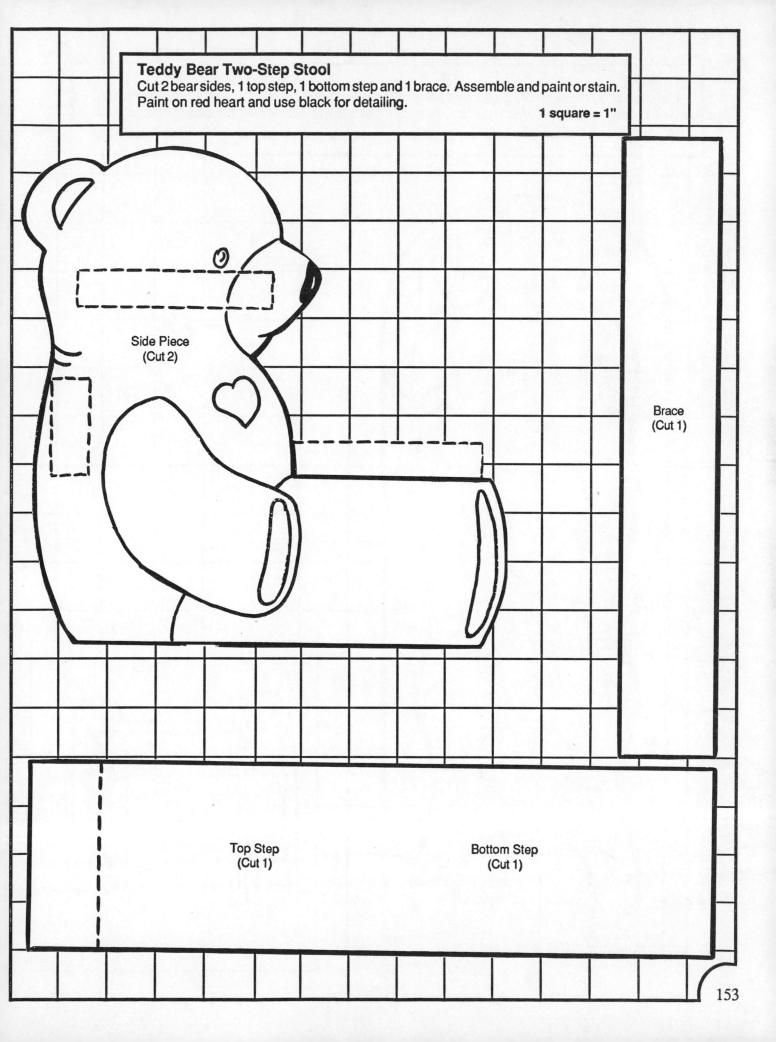

Teddy Bear Two-Step Stool
Cut 2 bear sides, 1 top step, 1 bottom step and 1 brace. Assemble and paint or stain. Paint on red heart and use black for detailing.

1 square = 1"

Side Piece
(Cut 2)

Brace
(Cut 1)

Top Step
(Cut 1)

Bottom Step
(Cut 1)

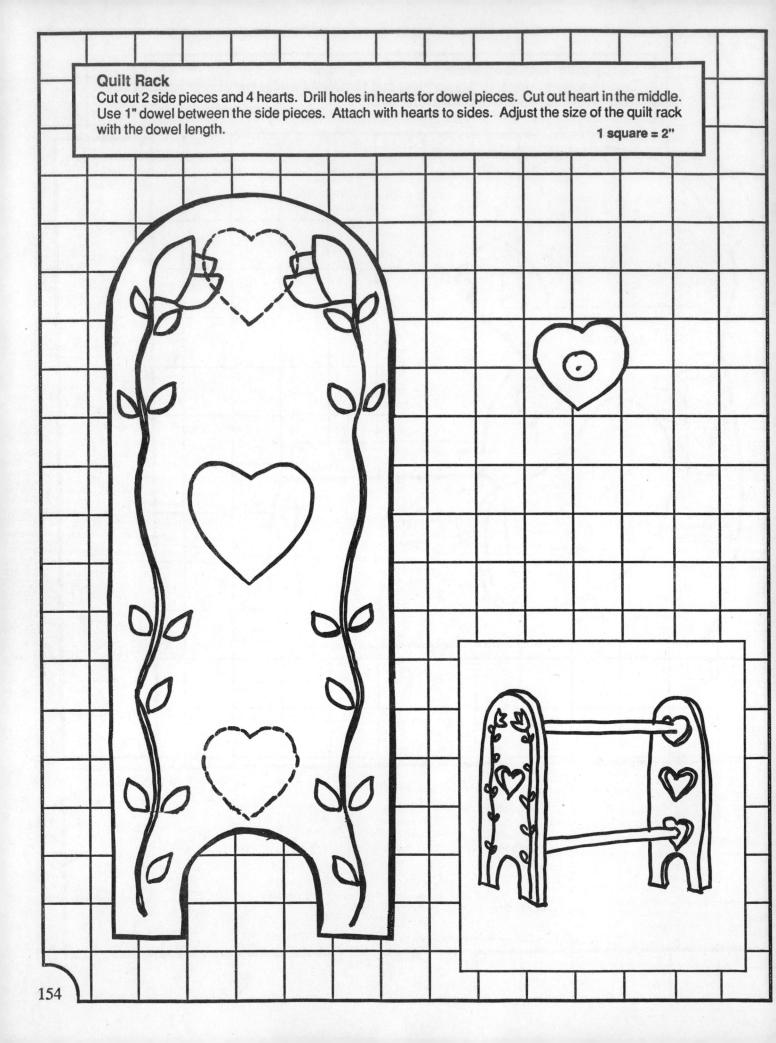

Quilt Rack
Cut out 2 side pieces and 4 hearts. Drill holes in hearts for dowel pieces. Cut out heart in the middle. Use 1" dowel between the side pieces. Attach with hearts to sides. Adjust the size of the quilt rack with the dowel length.

1 square = 2"

Indoor or Outdoor Window Box

Cut out 2 front/back pieces and 2 sides from pressure treated wood. Using pressure treated wood, cut out a bottom to make the box, allowing for sides. Make the box as wide as you need it. If your window is wider than this pattern, adjust the pattern and add as many flowers as you need. Cut flowers out separately, then attach (as shown). Assemble box and attach to window. Place name, House Number or "Welcome" on box front.

GRUEN

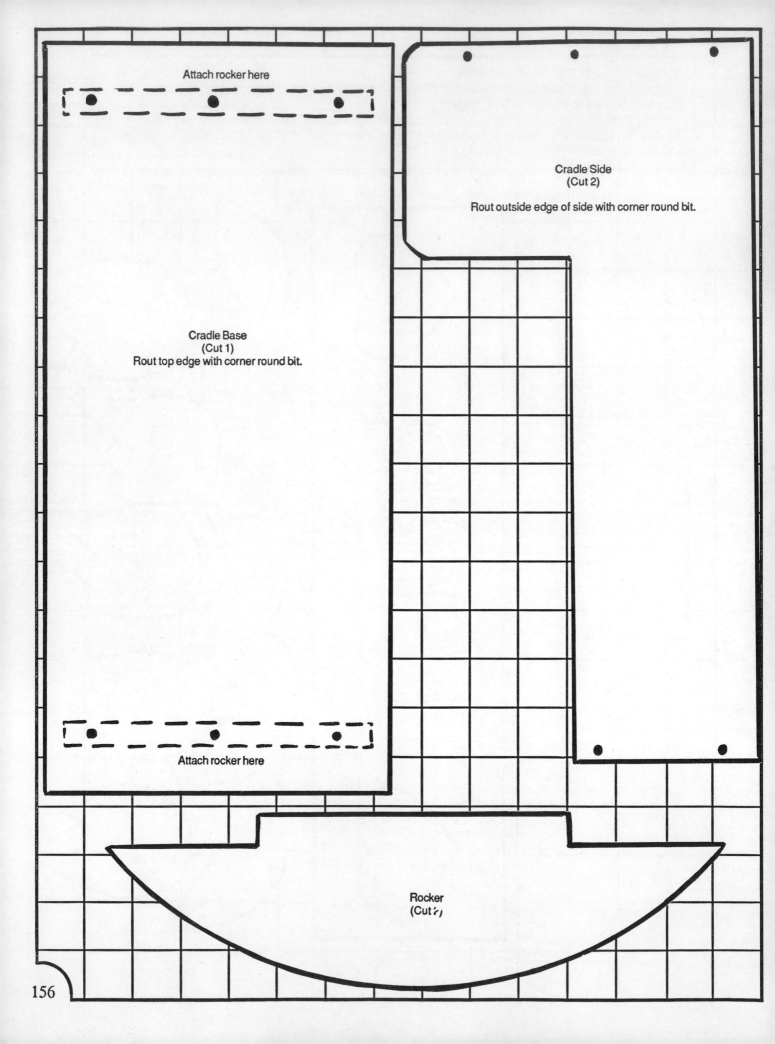

Attach rocker here

Cradle Base
(Cut 1)
Rout top edge with corner round bit.

Attach rocker here

Cradle Side
(Cut 2)

Rout outside edge of side with corner round bit.

Rocker
(Cut 2)

156

Child's Cradle

1 square = 1-1/2"

Material List
12' 1" x 12" pine #2 grade
26 #6 1 1/2" dry wall screws
yellow glue
sandpaper
finishing materials as desired.

Assembly Instructions

1. Cut out parts per pattern and sand. Outer edge of sides and top of rocker base should be routed before assembly.

2. Attach the 2 sides to end parts with glue and screws. This group should be assembled on a flat surface to insure correct contact to rocker base.

3. Attach rockers to base with glue and screws. Pattern shows attaching area. Screws attach through pre-drilled holes in top of rocker base.

4. Attach side and end assembly to base after two hours drying time. Screws enter from bottom of pre-drilled rocker base.

5. Cradle can now be finished as desired. Acrylic paint and stain can be coated with polyurethane to seal.

Head Board
(Cut 1)

Foot Board
(Cut 1)

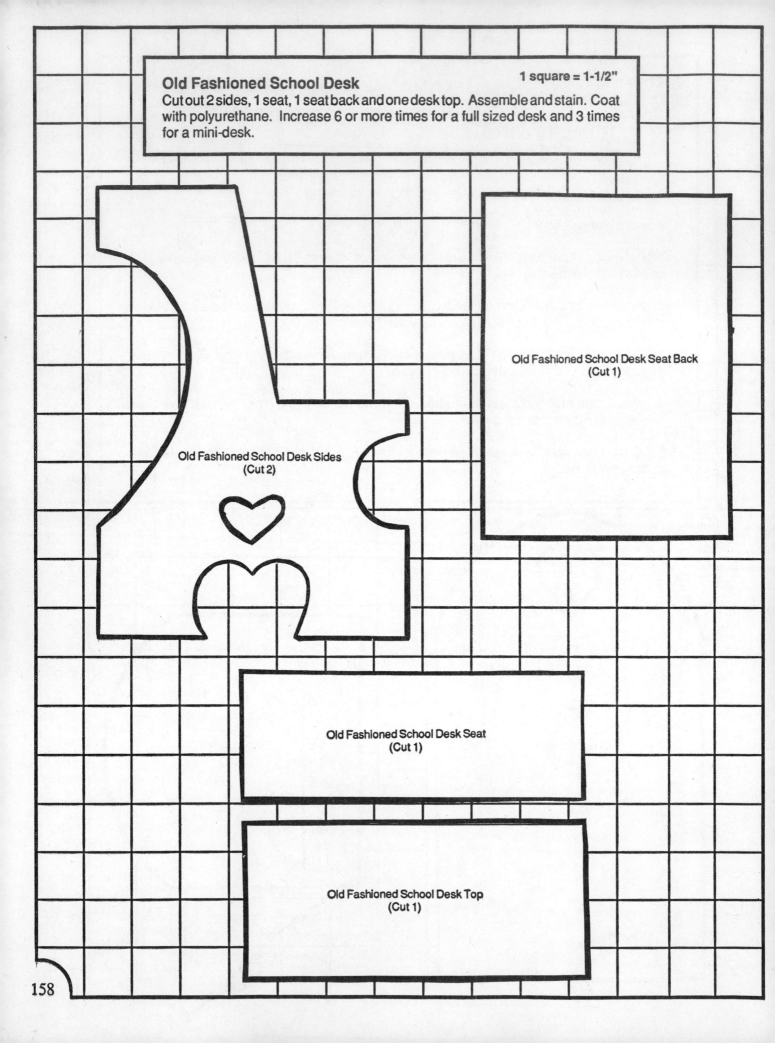

Old Fashioned School Desk
Cut out 2 sides, 1 seat, 1 seat back and one desk top. Assemble and stain. Coat with polyurethane. Increase 6 or more times for a full sized desk and 3 times for a mini-desk.

1 square = 1-1/2"

Old Fashioned School Desk Seat Back
(Cut 1)

Old Fashioned School Desk Sides
(Cut 2)

Old Fashioned School Desk Seat
(Cut 1)

Old Fashioned School Desk Top
(Cut 1)

Index

Alphabet
Name Plaque, 27
Acrylics, 8
Amish
Amish Doorstop, 125
An Amish Welcome, 10
Angels
Noel Banner, 70
Joy Tissue Box Cover, 72
Plaque, 71
Whirligig, 106
Apples
Basket Welcome, 11
Fruit Necklace, 36
Stool, 152
Balloons
Balloon Earrings, 32
Bananas
Fruit Necklace, 36
Band Saw, 6
Banks
Dinosaur Banks, 138, 139
Barn
Barn Mailbox , 148, 149
Door Harp, 93
Farmstyle Shelf, 128
Little Red Barn, 51, 52
Weather Vane, 101
Barrette Covers
Classy Southwestern Barrette
Cover , 29
Skater Barrette Cover
Holders, 31
Rapunzel Hair Clasp/
Ribbon Holder, 48
Baseball
Baseball Organizer, 89
Baskets
Watermelon Basket, 142
Bathroom Accessories, 113, 114
Bears
Bear Necklace, 36
Graduation Figure, 90
Hugging Bear Hang Up, 119
Joy Bear Plaque, 73
Miss Dancing Bear Mini-
Plaque, 61
Mr. Dancing Bear Mini-
Plaque, 61
Teddy Bear Stool, 153
Whirligig, 108
Zoo Menagerie Bears, 62
Belt Buckles
Circus Belt Buckle, 32
Classy Southwestern Belt
Buckle, 29
Christmas Belt Buckle, 34
Birds
Tern Yard Bird, 98
Toucan Yard Bird, 97
Birdhouses
Heart, Home Birdhouse, 99
Traditional Birdhouse, 100
Birthday
Candle Holders, 82, 83
Perpetual Calendar, 79, 80

Books
Book Lover's Plaque, 26
Bookends
Cabin Bookends, 132
Duck Book Rack, 133
Bows
Scottie, Bows Necklace, 36
Bow Tie Earrings, 34
Bow Tie Single Hole Tee-
Pull, 34
Brushes, 8
Bulletin Boards
Jack 'n Jill, 44
Bunnies: See Rabbits
Cake Toppers
Birthday Candle Holders, 82,
83
Calendars
Perpetual Calendar, 79, 80
Candle Holders
Birthday, 82, 83
Choir Boy Double Candle
Holder, 121
Elegant Candelabra, 122
Hearts 'n Ribbons Single
Candle Holder, 122
Tri-Stand Candle Holder, 121
Carbon paper, 7
Carrots
Bunny, Carrot Necklace, 36
Cat
Book Lover's Plaque, 26
Cat Crossing Outdoor Garden
Decoration, 103
Cozy Kitchen Welcome, 16
Farm Cat Stand Up Toy, 49
Peek-a-boo Shelf Sitter, 66
Playful Cat, 60
Whirligig, 108
Chickens
Hen Stand Up Toy, 50
Rooster Stand Up Toy, 50
Christmas
Angel Noel Banner, 70
Angel Plaque, 71
Canadian Goose Christmas
Greetings Wreath, 67
Country Christmas Sign, 69
Gift Ornaments, 75, 78
Joy Tissue Box Cover, 72
Joy Bear Plaque, 73
Novelty Multi-Sided
Christmas Tree, 74
Old Fashioned Santa Wall
Plaque, 68
Twelve Days of Christmas
Ornament Set, 76, 77
Rudolph Fashion Jewelry
Ensemble, 34
Snowflake, 75
Stair-Step Mr. & Mrs.
Claus, 78
Wise Men Jewelry, 35
Yard Soldier, 70
Circus
Circus Jewelry, 32

Circus Play Set, 53-58
Clamps, 7
Clocks
Clock Shelf, 37
Contemporary Clock, 42
Hickory Dickory Dock
Clock, 43
Kitchen Cookie Jar Clock, 40
City Hall Clock, 37
Welcome Heart Clock, 39
Clowns
Big Top Jewelry, 32
Circus Play Set, 53
Coat Racks: See Peg Racks
Cows
Cow Stand Up Toy, 50
Cow Weather Vane, 10
Holstein Cow on a Base, 61
Noah's Cow Earrings, 33
Paper Towel Holder, 109
Cradle, 156, 157
Desk, 158
Dinosaurs
Dinosaur Banks, 138, 139
Graduation Figure, 91
Dogs
Lazy Dog Farm Toy, 50
Mad Dog Earrings, 31
Mad Dog T-Pull, 30
Scottie, Bows Necklace, 36
Sitting Dog Farm Toy, 49
Door Harps, 93-96
Door Stops
Amish Doorstop, 125
Country Pig Doorstop, 126
Shell Motif Doorstop, 124
Dove
Dove Scarf Slide, 33
Peace Dove in Flight, 88
Drills, 6
Ducks
Book Rack, 133
Country Christmas Sign, 69
Door Harp, 94
Duck Coat Rack, 116
Duck House Sign, 13
Duck Weather Vane, 101
Easy 3-D Duck Plaque, 22
Farm Duck Stand Up Toy, 50
Paper Towel Holder, 110
Eagles
Plaques, 20, 21
Earrings: See Jewelry
Easter
For God So Loved the World
Plaque, 87
Easter Rabbit on Stand, 86
Perpetual Calendar, 79, 80
Elephant
Zoo Menagerie, 62, 63
Enlargement, 6, 7
Fairy Tales & Nursery Rhymes
Hickory Dickory Dock
Clock, 43
Jack-Jill Bulletin Board, 44
Little Bo Peep Shelf, 46

Rapunzel Hair Clasp/Ribbon
Holder, 48
Rub-A-Dub-Dub Bathroom
Multi-Purpose Peg, 45
Tortoise & Hare Shelf, 47
Farm
Farm Play Set, 49-52
Farmers
Farmer Toy, 49
Farmer's Wife Toy, 49
Fireplace Insert, 115
Fish
Fish Hanger, 90
Flowers
Basket, 115
Iris, 84
Tulip, 84, 113, 114, 155
Morning Glory, 84
Daffodils, 85
Daisies, 85
Flowers and Planter, 84, 85
Garden Ornaments: See Yard
Ornaments
Geese
A Gaggle of Geese, 64
Canadian Goose Greetings
Wreath, 67
Canadian Goose on Stand, 86
Farm Goose Toy, 49
Wistful Goose, 21
Giraffe
Zoo Menagerie, 63
Gnomes
Gnome Whimsical Window
Sill Decorations, 120
Goats
Farm Goat Toy, 50
Graduation
Graduation Figures, 90, 91
Grandmas
Grandma Stand Up Toy, 49
Grandpas
Grandpa Stand Up Toy, 49
Grapes
Fruit Necklace, 36
Graph paper, 6,7
Hangers: See Peg Racks/Hangers
Heart
Carousel Horse on Heart, 59
Country Clock Shelf, 37
Double Heart House Sign, 12
Front Door Number Sign, 18
Heart, Home Birdhouse, 99
Hearts 'n Ribbons Single
Candle Holder, 122
Peg-Of-My-Heart Multi-
Purpose Rack, 118
Heart Corner Shelf, 127
Twisted Heart Stool, 150
Welcome Heart, 39
Hens
Farm Hen Stand Up Toy, 50
Hippopotamus
Zoo Menagerie, 62
Horses
Carousel Horse on Heart, 59

Horse Weather Vane, 101
Oats for Sale Peg Rack, 117
Plow Horse Decoration, 65
Independence Day
Uncle Sam Figure, 92
Perpetual Calendar, 79, 80
Jesus
For God So Loved the World
Plaque, 87
Jewelry
Bear Necklace, 36
Bunny, Carrot Necklace, 36
Circus Jewelry Ensemble, 32
Classy Southwestern
Jewelry, 29, 30
Far-Out Contemporary
Jewelry, 30, 31
Fruit Necklace, 36
Noah's Ark Jewelry, 33
Rudolph Jewelry, 34
Scottie, Bows Necklace, 36
Wise Men Jewelry, 35
Jig Saw, 6
Kangaroo
Toy Toss, 140
Kitchen
Accessories, 109-112
Cozy Kitchen Welcome, 16
Kitchen Canning Welcome,
17
Kitchen Cookie Jar Clock, 40
Lambs: See Sheep
Lemons
Fruit Necklace, 36
Letter Holders
Combination Letter/Key/
Message Holder, 146
U.S. Mail Letter Holder, 147
Lions: See Circus
Zoo Menagerie, 63
Luan, 6
Magazine Racks
Portable Magazine Rack, 144
Tulip Magazine/Newspaper
Rack, 145
Vertical Rack, 143
Mailboxes
Country Barn Mailbox
Cover, 148, 149
Mice
3-D Mouse, 60
Milk Cans
Milk Can Plaque, 25
Mobiles
End of the Rainbow/St.
Patrick's Day, 81
Modern
Classy Southwestern
Jewelry, 29, 30
Clock, 42
Far-Out Contemporary
Jewelry, 30, 31
Ultraman Sculpture, 41
Necklaces: See Jewelry
Noah's Ark
Noah's Ark Jewelry, 33
Numbers/Numerals
Birthday Candle Holders, 82,
83
Perpetual Calendar, 79, 80
Nursery Rhymes & Fairy Tales
Hickory Dickory Dock
Clock, 43
Jack-Jill Bulletin Board, 44

Little Bo Peep Shelf, 46
Rapunzel Hair Clasp/Ribbon
Holder, 48
Rub-A-Dub-Dub Bathroom
Multi-Purpose Peg, 45
Tortoise & Hare Shelf, 47
Oranges
Fruit Necklace, 36
Owls
Barn Owl Stand Up Farm
Toy, 49
Painting, 7, 8
Pantograph, 6
Paper Towel Holders, 109, 110
Particle board, 6
Peg Racks/Hangers
Duck Coat Rack, 116
Fish Hanger/Rack, 90
Hugging Bear Hang Ups, 119
Oats for Sale Peg Rack, 117
Peg-Of-My-Heart Multi-
Purpose Rack, 118
Rub-A-Dub-Dub Bathroom
Multi-Purpose Peg, 45
Southwestern Design
Signs, 14, 15
Photocopy, 7
Pine, 6
Pigs
Country Pig Doorstop, 126
Hog Weather Vane, 102
Paper Towel Holder, 109
Sitting Pig Farm Toy, 49
Lazy Pig Farm Toy, 50
Pins: See Jewelry
Plant Stands, 134, 135
Planter Box
Weaver's "Camel" Planters
Box, 141
Plaques
Angel Noel Banner, 70
Angel Plaque, 71
Book Lover's Plaque, 26
Comedy, Tragedy Plaque, 19
Country School Girl, 92
Dancing Bear Mini-Plaques,
61
Eagle Plaques, 20, 21
Easy 3-D Duck Plaque, 22
For God So Loved the
World, 87
Joy Bear Plaque, 73
Mexican Pitcher, 23
Milk Can, 25
Name Plaques, 27
Old Fashioned Santa, 68
Peace Dove in Flight, 88
Sack o' Corn Meal, 24
Victorian Lady & Gent, 28
Plywood, 6
Polyurethane, 8
Rabbits
Bunny, Carrot Necklace, 36
Easter Rabbit on Stand, 86
Rabbit Farm Toy, 50
Tortoise & Hare Shelf, 47
Racks: See Peg Racks
Rainbow
Circular Rainbow Tee-Shirt
Knotter, 33
Rainbow Mobile, 81
Reduction, 6, 7
Roosters
Crowing Rooster Toy, 50

Safety goggles, 5
Sanding, 6, 7
Santas
Old Fashioned Santa, 68
Stair-Step Mr. & Mrs.
Claus, 78
Scarecrows
Garden Decoration, 104
Scarf Slides
Classy Southwestern, 30
Frankincense, 35
Good News Dove, 33
Popcorn, 32
Skater, 31
Sconces
Country Sconce, 129
Southwestern Design Shelf/
Sconce, 131
Scroll saw, 6
Shadowboxes
Rocket Shadowbox, 130
Sheep
Country Lamb on Stand, 65
Door Harp, 96
Little Bo Peep Shelf, 46
Sheep Plant Stand, 135
Sheep Stand Toy, 50
Shells
Shell Motif Doorstop, 124
Shelves
Country Heart Clock Shelf,
37
Farm-Style Corner Shelf, 128
Heart Corner Shelf, 127
Little Bo Peep Shelf, 46
Sitters
Peek-a-boo Cat Shelf
Sitter, 66
Stair-Step Mr. & Mrs.
Claus, 78
Tortoise & Hare Shelf, 47
Uncle Sam Figure, 92
Signs
Baby's Sleeping Doorknob
Hanging
Duck House Sign, 13
Front Door House Number
Sign, 18
Double Heart House Sign, 12
Southwestern House Sign, 15
Welcome Friends Tavern-
Style Sign, 9
Skunks
Skunk Farm Toy, 50
Snowflakes
Snowflake, 75
Soldiers
Christmas Ornament, 75
Soldier Yard Ornament, 70
Southwestern
Classy Southwestern
Jewelry, 29, 30
Mexican Pitcher Plaque, 23
Southwestern Signs, 14, 15
Southwestern Design Shelf,
131
Southwestern Stool, 151
St. Patrick's Day
End of the Rainbow Mobile,
81
Perpetual Calendar, 79, 80
Staining, 8
Steel wool, 7
Stencilling, 8

Stools
Apple One-Step Stool, 152
Southwestern Stool, 151
Teddy Bear Two-Step Stool,
153
Twisted Heart Stool, 150
Switchplates
Single Switchplates, 137
Tissue Box Covers
Joy Tissue Box Cover, 72
Tole painting, 8
Tools, 5-8
Toys
Circus Play Set, 53-58
Farm Play Set, 49-52
Tracing paper, 7
Train
Circus Train, 56-58
Transferring patterns, 6, 7
Tee-Shirt Pulls
Circular Rainbow Tee-Shirt
Knotter, 33
Classy Southwestern Tee-
Pull, 30
Clown T-Shirt Knotter, 32
Mad Dog T-Pull, 30
Rudolph Bow Tie Tee-Pull,
34
Wise Man Tee-Pull, 35
Tulips: See Flowers
Tung oil, 8
Turkeys
Turkey Farm Toy, 50
Turtles
Plant Stand, 134
Tortoise & Hare Shelf, 47
Uncle Sam
Uncle Sam Figure, 92
Victorian
Lady & Gent, 28
Video Organizers
Video Cassette Holders, 123
Watermelons
Watermelon Basket, 142
Weather Vanes
Deluxe Weather Vanes, 101,
102
Whirligigs
Angel, 106
Bear, 108
Cat, 108
Washwoman, 107
Windmill, 105
Windmills
Whirligig, 105
Wood, 6
Wreaths
Canadian Goose Christmas
Greetings Wreath, 67
Yard Ornaments
Cat Crossing Garden
Decoration, 103
Scarecrow Herb Garden
Decoration, 104
Uncle Sam Figure, 92
Weather Vanes: See Weather
Vanes
Yard Birds, 97, 98
Yard Soldier, 70
Zoo
Menagerie Animals, 62, 63
3-D, 6